THROUGH THE
EYES OF A COP

THROUGH THE EYES OF A COP

Allan A. Cimino

iUniverse, Inc.
Bloomington

Through the Eyes of a Cop

iUniverse books may be ordered through booksellers or by contacting:

iUniverse
1663 Liberty Drive
Bloomington, IN 47403
www.iuniverse.com
1-800-Authors (1-800-288-4677)

ISBN: 978-1-4759-4188-3 (sc)
ISBN: 978-1-4759-4242-2 (hc)
ISBN: 978-1-4759-4189-0 (ebk)

Library of Congress Control Number: 2012913782

Printed in the United States of America

iUniverse rev. date: 08/03/2012

DEDICATIONS

To my Field Training Officer, Bobby Di Paolo, I hope I spelt your name right. Who showed me how to treat people with respect, neat as a pin, got dirty when he had to. I always kept that in mind.

To my first partners on the job: Joe Birro

To my friend Artie Boor who became my friend and mentor at one of the toughest Precincts in the city. The conversations we had just to get into a different world other then crime. And who gave me my first workout program, which I still use today. Thanks for being there.

To the Police Officers I have worked with male and female, and the ones paying attention over the air, who knew I might need a back up, even if I didn't ask for one, and the ones watching out for me.

The bosses who made me feel okay, and we became friends, because in their hearts they were still cops, and knew one when they saw one.

Wayne Konje: Port Authority Police Office, who received the Medal of Valor, and whom I met through my ex wife's family. He lived in New Jersey.

Bill Kaiser: Who heard one of my stories and it did not fall to deaf ears. He was an investigator for the New York Phone Company, and I never knew it, set me up with a wire tap. And who was married to my friend Ann, now known as Ann Brown.

And all the other Cops and Bosses who are still doing their job under all types of adversity.

It was my pleasure to have worked with many good Police Officers. Thanks for being there.

SPECIALS THANKS

To Pat Logudice Matarazzo, Who responded to a question I asked her over the net. With that she offered me her help, with correcting and checking for grammar errors, typing over some of the pages. She explained how Microsoft worked, and answering many questions that I asked, giving me her answers and repeating her answers when they weren't getting through to me.

At the time, I hit a brick wall, and felt like I was blocked, she gave me the incentive to start getting my rear in gear and move forward again with my writings and completing this book, every time I stopped, I thought of her, and "hey when". Sometimes you need someone around, to clear your road up a bit. The communicating over the net did just that for me. Thanks again.

There's another special friend who I would like to thank. His name is Joseph Iacone Jr. Who was a New York City Police Officer. This guy changed the direction of my life, by being a good friend and for his help in getting me to become a Police Officer. If it wasn't for him I don't know where I would have ended up today, not a good place. This is a special thanks to this person I will never forget. also his family, his father Joseph, mother Mary, his two brother's Carl, and Sal a New York City Decoy Transit Detective, in helping me get through some of the hard times when my mother was sick and dying.

I remember one day when I was around eight or nine years of age. It was a summer day, the kitchen window was open, the breeze was blowing in and the sheer curtains that were on the window were blowing around.

My mother's was in bed, she was rushed to the hospital the night before, she had gauze in her nose, and well I was cooking my famous fried chicken. I guess at that age all my cooking was famous and hopefully eatable. Well the oil from the frying pan either splashed or the curtains hit the flame, all of a sudden the curtains are in flames, my mother saw this and starts screaming, Joe Sr. was home heard the screams, ran into my house pulled the curtains from the window, threw them in the sink and opened the faucet, I didn't know what to do, he smiled at me, took them with him and left. Mary was always at the window when I did my cooking, looking across and smiling. Things you don't forget. With love to you all.

THROUGH THE EYES OF A COP

October 1, 1973, one of the, if not, best days of my life, becoming a New York City Police Officer. I remember going to the Police Academy on 20th street between 2nd avenue and 3rd avenue, in Manhattan, walking from the train station, up to the Police Academy, and looking at the building. Never feeling, any prouder than that day, and never thinking I'd be here.

We were assigned to companies and instructors. I was in company 53? We were the first class that year to get out of the gray uniforms and into, blue shirts and dark pants. I think it was a relief. The grays were to outstanding for people who knew nothing about the law or being a police officer, Or being in the public eye without any knowledge of what was going on. The blues were I think a little more concealing when you traveled on Public transportation, a little more relaxing, if you get my drift.

I'm sure our company had the two best Instructors at the academy, by the way they taught and because of all the complaints you heard from the other trainees about their instructors. You would hear about one of the instructors; he was teaching and giving the wrong information, just before one of the important tests. This guy, the rumor was, doing undercover narcotics; they took him off the street, for some reason, and made him an instructor. The two instructors we had, one a police officer, the other a sergeant, they seemed like they really wanted to teach and make you pass. It looked as if they put their heart and soul into it. The police instructor, called one of the girl trainee, big tits, she had a nice set, I figure he was getting her ready for the street, and you knew either a police officer or some jerk was, sooner or later going to make that remark, so you better get used to it. You can't get mad or fight every time someone says it. So let it roll off your shoulder.

Another one of the girls that was in the company, I spoke to, said she and her husband or her friend owned some concessions in Coney Island, in Brooklyn. Just by looking at her and her demeanor, you just knew, she didn't take any shit. Don't get me wrong, she was attractive, she just looked like she could handle herself. Street smart and she proved it on the Police Academy stage.

They were having a play act, of a family dispute; they picked her and another person. I don't remember if the other rookie was male or female. They said family disputes and car stops are the most dangerous, because they're unpredictable. Well anyway, she's up there and the tenants of the so called apartment are yelling and screaming, I guess the two police officers were in an awkward position. All the trainees, the bosses the head of the academy were watching them. The big thing was, make sure you're a professional. Well these two tenants were going off, her partner was trying to keep them separated, she look a little gun shy, they were still yelling and trying to go at each other, when all of a sudden, the one I'm was talking about from Coney island. She came out, she started yelling and took charge, the audience went ape shit, started clapping and yelling for her, after that, we knew that was her and she was a good piece of work.

There were these two guys in our class. Their main objective was to get out on three quarters. Don't get me wrong, nice guys one was serious dry sense of humor, the other sort of a class clown, I don't remember if one or both of them got what they wanted. I remember being, whether, it was the 61 precinct or 63 precinct. I was on patrol, on a four by twelve shift. It was raining hard that night, when we spot this Cadillac going through reds lights. We put light and sirens on, for a car stop. He starts to run, we put it over the air, in pursuit, we hit some nice speeds especially for that type of night. All these things start going through your mind, G.L.A, [stolen auto] robbery suspect, drugs, gun and so on. All of a sudden the car pulls into the curbs, who do you think gets out of the car, with a big grin on his face, but, you got it, class clown. He though it was a big joke. I looked at him; you knew that if you explained what a fucking idiot he was, putting us in danger of a car accident, he wouldn't understand. I looked at him, just shook my head, 91 central, proper I D.

GETTING BACK TO THE ACADEMY

The two instructors that we had, made the learning interesting, made us feel like, we wanted to become cops. Don't get me wrong, for a guy like me, out of school 7 years, and I never liked school. I had to study three to four hours a day, just to absorb the work. I had to take pages and pages of notes, while this one guy in class, took almost no notes, he kept his notes in is top shirt pocket, smart guy, not bad. My girlfriend at the time who was going to college, taught me how to organize and underline the important facts with a yellow magic marker, how to use acronyms. She tested me plenty, in more ways than one, sometimes I'd passed sometimes I'd fail; she was a big help for me in passing my tests.

I remember walking from the academy to the train station with a few of the guys I used to pal out with. This female, I don't know if she was drunk or on drugs, came up to us and called us pigs. All of us we were taken off guard probably startled a bit. We looked at each other, the only thing we could do was laugh. But I think deep down, I know, for me, it made an impression. Still thinking like a civilian at the time. Just because of the clothes we were wearing, and then out of nowhere, this came. That might have been a good experience. Because I thought, we were in for a lot more and worse . . . I think that started self control for me. Another time near the academy, I was on one side the street. I noticed a police officer on the corner and a young boy from behind pointed a toy gun at him, so when he turned around there was this boy with a gun. I guess it takes a split second to sizing up a situation, another impression. All these impressions were put to use during my twenty years on patrol. You're going to come across this and much more . . .

From the academy, I use to hang out with one of the guys in the class. Real nice guy, he had a girlfriend. His girlfriend and mine hit it off well. I use to go with him to his neighborhood, and play handball. The court was like almost under the Verrazano Bridge. We went on vacation with them. He was telling me his girl got a job in Manhattan, managing the Gap. One time he was talking to her on the phone at her job. When he heard her whole demeanor change, he asked her if there's trouble she said yes, I don't remember if he asked her if it is a robbery.

He hung up, he was in Brooklyn, called 911 reported a problem at her location, told them who he was. He hung up and headed for the city. When the police got to her place, they bagged a guy. He was going to, or was in the process of doing a robbery. She wasn't hurt. They ended up getting married and buying a house on Staten Island. We went there once or twice double dated, and we parted friends.

The gym class, I think, might have been four hours a day. It was great, again except for the class clowns. I guess every company had its clown. Every time someone would talk or made some kind of remark, we had to do the duck walk. Squat down and walk around the gym, one instructor really enjoyed this punishment. With him, anything off beat and there was the duck walk. He was a real ball buster, I think; the instructors wanted the class, to take care of these guys.

We did boxing. One of the gym instructors, they called Mr. Clean, you know bald head, tall and they said he used to box. He would walk around, and correct us, our stance, our hands, with me, he stopped, told me to throw a few punches at his hands, and then he went to look for the next person. Another instructor was a black belt. The rumor was when he was on the street, he didn't take any shit, and that he stuffed some guy down a sewer. He looked like the type to; again, take no shit, another impression. Sometimes, you have to do, what you have to do. We were taught self defense, against knives, guns, and were taught how to use the night stick and Billy club, it was a small hard rubber object, around eleven inches long. It was kept in rear pocket, for close strikes, real good for getting a point across, for most stubborn people, who don't understand the English language.

Some thought that some of the girls were getting special treatment. I'm pretty sure they were. There was one girl, who wasn't to popular, she was getting over with her looks and her flirting, you could tell, by looking at the other girl trainees, that they didn't like it either. At that time we were learning how to throw a person and take him or her down and learning to fall. The one that was not to popular, she was not too far from where I was training. This one guy flipped her, and I mean flipped her, where I thought her head raddled, from the look on her face, I think she got the drift, I did feel sorry for her, I think he did it a little too hard, what can I say, maybe hormones took control.

We did arm twirls for quite some time. Arm twirls are, you extend your arms out full length, and make small circles with them. After they told us the reason, we understood. They said, when you have your gun out on a perp, and you're by yourself, waiting for your backup to come that weapon becomes pretty heavy in that kind of a situation. No more said. We also did stop and frisk. That's when you have a perp, or possibly perps. You have him up against a wall and you're going to pat him down for weapons or anything that can be used as a weapon, or drugs etc.

The instructor said make sure you pat his head, possibly for razors or hand cuff keys, especially if he or she has an afro or real thick or long hair. With this you have to be careful, especially for dirty needles, something that can cause a sickness. You make sure you grab his groin, again for guns or other weapons. It was my turn, and at that time I still had this shyness, so when we did the pat downs, I know I patted him down a little timidly, this instructor starts screaming at me, that's not the way you toss a guy, if it was up to me, I'd throw you out of the academy. I just starred and looked at him. He said nothing. Nice, I needed this, more fucking baggage to carry. But he was right, life or death, your choice. Or the next police officer that deals with this guy or female because of a bad frisk can get killed or hurt.

We did the run around the gym, to get us to build up to the mile and a half. There use to be stairs in the gym that lead down to the locker rooms. So as we were doing the running, I would spot a few of the trainees, as they were about to pass the stairs, before the run was over, duck and head down the steps to the locker room where there's a will there's a way, hey to each his own.

The firing range, another big day for me, here's where we were taught to fire a firearm. This was the first time I handled a weapon. There were two instructors, one white guy and one black guy. The black guy another rumor just, he came out of I.A.D. (internal affairs division) me personally, I couldn't give a shit, then or now, if he was doing his job that's his job, case closed.

The first guy teaching us the weapons the white police officer. All technical jargon, I couldn't understand a thing he was saying. I'd get up to the booth, put my goggles on, put the target up, shoot like shit, low seventies, again more pressure, you have to pass or no guns. Another tech talk from the white police officer, again, no go for me. As I was about to shoot again, the black instructor takes me on the side, he says, this is what you got to do, see these sights, in front, I said yea, see those two points in back, yea, you have to make sure that the point in front is in the middle of those two points in back with the same space on both sides and make all three level, I said that's what he was trying to tell me, he said yea.

Just to take it off course. The same thing happened when I took a short course in flying a helicopter. The course was given to me by my ex as a birthday present. I had to go to Manhattan. I'm in the room or class, this guy is talking about how to fly, I'm there sitting, not understanding a word he's saying, everyone's taking notes all listening to all the tech, I'm with this other guy. So the instructor, he's looking at me, so he doesn't want me to feel like a shit, so indirectly, and I know he's talking to me, he's says all you have to do is this, this and this. Boom a light goes on, so that's' what he's talking about. I go to New Jersey, and flew a helicopter. Some instructors, have class and others, try. Great feeling, looking at the Statue of Liberty's torch, eye to eye.

We had a shooting contest, one group against another. They needed around six shooters for each group, some of the other people in the class wanted me to be in the contest, so I entered, I don't know if we won or lost but according to a few of the guys in class, they said I shot number one for the class. I never checked it out, yea, I felt good. Nice guy. Thanks. That was for the black training police officer.

Back to the gym, for testing day. I don't remember, you had to do a certain amount of laps around the gym to pass, I don't know if it was a mile or a mile and a half, well I was really struggling with it. You know before this day, in the gym doing all the work outs, than for the break, up to the second floor promenade to see how many cigarettes you can get in before the break was over, yea, good for the breathing. Well I was having a rough time. This guy in my class, either he saw me or he could tell I was at my last breath, as I was going to pass him, he started yelling, hey Al what are you doing you did enough laps, I stopped . . . again, another save, thanks . . . passed. I met him one more time after the academy.

The day of the last written test was nerve racking. Waiting for the marks, I think when the marks came down. One or two persons in our class failed, you felt bad for them, and I don't know if they held them over, whether they were going to do a makeover test or dismiss them.

The big day was Shield day in the auditorium, another proud day. As they were calling out names to pick up your shield, one police officer, from our class was called out of the ceremony. Rumor says, something came back on his investigation that might have been a no, no. I don't know if he was dismissed, held over or what. The inspector of the academy made a speech. That I know touched me, and I'm sure others. He told us to look at ourselves as professionals. He compared us to lawyers, doctors and others.

And I know that was a big turning point in my life, as how I would present myself, as a professional police officer. Another point of info, in the Police Department, the rumors flow like water, some true some bullshit, just to make someone look like shit. If I was interested in a rumor, my thing was. "When in doubt check it out."

From there we bought our uniforms, service revolvers and off duty revolver. The off duty was either a Smith and Wesson or a Colt. The Colt was a six shooter, the smith a five. The Colt a little bigger than the Smith, I took the Colt, why not have the extra bullets. We were given our first precinct assignments. My first precinct was the 61precinct, Avenue U and East 14 street Brooklyn, Brooklyn South Area.

The only person that attended the ceremony with me was my girlfriend, no family.

After the ceremony in which, at the time Mayor Beam, gave us a speech, we found out later two police officers, I guess, got carried away with the excitement, went into the bar across the street from the Academy and had a few drinks, in uniform, again a no no, were caught and dismissed. They probably got caught up in the moment. Before that another two were caught playing with a Frisbee over the Brooklyn Bridge in academy uniforms, again rumor dismissed.

BROOKLYN SOUTH

Brooklyn South Area, consisted of the 60—precinct, 61-precinct 63-precinct maybe the 69-precinct and 67, they are huge precincts in area. As you go further north on Flatbush Avenue the precincts get heavier or the crime is higher. The 61 there were mostly burglaries and G.L.A.'s, {grand larceny autos} tons of paperwork and reports. Somewhat important people in some of the areas, politically connected.

We were supposed to be assigned to F.T.O.'s which stood for Field Training Officers. I didn't get one the first night, so I was hooked up with a veteran cop. We were assigned to East Kings Highway, around East 15th street. We took the train to our post, got off at the station, went downstairs, and went outside. The first thing he says, "Ok kid, what do you want to do"? "Hang out in the firehouse or go to the movies, "now I'm a new kid on the block, so I tell him, hey look, I came here to be a cop, not to hang out in these places.

I'm not going to the firehouse or the movies, you want to go, than go, he looked at me, said nothing, we walked around. I guess, my first impression that I made, I guess wasn't too good and there would be many more to come. I don't think we talked all night, which was ok. At that time, I didn't like to talk anyway.

After that I was assigned to a field training officer, at the time a field training officer would have a detective shield worn on his uniform. My guy was a white shield F.T.O. with the promise that he would eventually receive the gold shield. This guy was a dapper, well dressed, outgoing personality, an actor, totally opposite of me.

Before being a police officer he was in a singing group. I think it was Vito and the Salutations. Their big hit song was Gloria, and he would say, "the slow version," and he'd start singing it; also, he was a ladies' man. He was the perfect guy for me, willing to teach, the right way. Taught me a lot, like the Jewish word Crepe-lock, he'd say "say it with a drool," I started laughing. He taught me plenty about how to act as a professional, and the way to treat people. He made a long lasting impression. Real pleasant and easy going guy to be with.

We were doing a four by twelve, going to a location, possible D.O.A. when we got there, a young boy between the age of ten and twelve answered the door, he looked scared. We went in, there was his mother on the bed, she looked like she was dead, my F.T.O. jumped on her and started to give her C.P.R. But from what I saw it was too late, I'm sure he knew, but he tried and it might have made an impression on her young son.

Another four by twelve with him, disorderly guy. When we got to the location, there was this loud mouth drunk, ready to Fight, so he tackles him, I'm standing there, he's on the ground with him, he yells get your cuffs out and cuff him, I cuff him, this guy was giving us a hard time. So when we're in the R.M.P, radio car, he tells me why was I just standing there, I said it was a fair fight, still thinking me, as a civilian. He says you're a cop there's no fair fights you jump in, I felt like shit, said nothing he never brought it up.

When we got him to the house, we took him into the detectives holding cell, this guy was still bad mouthing. Telling my field training officer, if you didn't have that gun I'd kick the shit out of you, so my partner, takes off his gun, goes into the cell and puts the loud mouth to sleep. Hey you were looking for a sedative, he gave you what one . . . two.

With my field training officer, I got my first free meal. He would walk into a supermarket, take two steaks or chops and walk out without paying, and he'd smile at the people who were working there, me, I just followed him. With me it didn't feel right, because all my life, I was taught, no one is going to give you anything for nothing, you want it, you work for it, you buy it, it's yours. But with him he must have been doing this a long time because the workers said hi and they smiled. I'm not saying it was wrong, but I knew then it was not for me. Then he would go into one of his favorite restaurants in Sheepshead Bay, give them the food, and he'd tell them when he would be back for dinner. They would cook it; serve us with all the vegetables and dessert and coffee, or espresso. We'd leave a tip. And again, it wasn't for me. With him I went along with the program, until I was on my own. Like I said, he was a big influence on my becoming the kind of police officer I was, through my entire career as a cop.

Throughout my career as a police officer I came across a lot of things that took me off guard, because it happened so fast or I knew nothing of it, or even put it in my mind that this could or would happen to me, as for me, when the time comes these are the rules, and your rules that you work by.

I remember on a four by twelve there was this chase in another precinct, it was coming over the air, they were chasing a Jaguar, and it might have been the adjacent precinct. On this job, I was working with another young rookie, who later was to become my partner. He came from the jails; he was a Correction Officer, before being a Police Officer. So we decided to tag along for the chase, the police officer's that were doing the chasing, the recorder was doing an excellent job giving the directions, east on this, west on that, south so and so forth, so you had a few precincts joining in, we were in the 61precinct, the Jaguar was caught and surrounded at Prospect Park by a number of radio cars from different precincts. Good coordinating nice job, no one got hurt. "One under."

The roll-call cop, an old timer asked me if I wanted to be a Unit Training Officer. A Unit Training Officer was a police officer, who would give a class at precinct level, about anything new or some new procedure that came up. I told him thanks, but no thanks, I just got on the job, and I wanted to do the street. Thanks

Another time we're driving around it was a midnight tour. Coney Island Avenue we're going east bound on one of the avenues. A car coming from the west on the same avenue, he makes a left onto Coney island avenue, his headlight were blinking so we made a car stop. The same young rookie as myself [correction officer]. The driver had slurred speech, three guys were in the car including the driver, we put a check on the plate, plate come back stolen, he says he borrowed the car without telling the family member that owned it, they reported it stolen. We searched the car and came up with bottles of some type of drugs that were under the seat. No one owned up to whose drugs they were, so everyone was arrested. One guy was so wasted, he couldn't talk. I took the collar, did the paperwork at Central Booking, this was the procedure at the time, years later it changed. I put them in the holding pen. I didn't realize that the amount of drugs they took would start taking effect on them, while I was going to talk to the A.D.A., (assistant district attorney). This one police officer that worked there came up to me and said one of my prisoners is convulsing or dying, nice, I needed this wake-up call. I ask him, did anyone call a bus {ambulance} he says no, not my problem, fucking hump. From there I took the prisoner to the hospital. I don't know if they pumped him or gave him something. When I brought him back to Central Booking, I talked to the A.D.A., remember I was still a rookie, you're still unsure not knowing if you're doing the right thing . . . After talking to the A.D.A., I waited for the wagon.

The wagon is the truck that transports the prisoners down to the Arraignment's Court holding cells. I rode with the driver. I took them down to 120 Schmouhorn Street to the holding pens. So if it was a four by twelve shift Tuesday, I'm into Wednesday, now it's a waiting game, and when I'm down at court I don't like to sleep. There's was a room where you can take a cat nap, or sleep until they called you. I'd walked around or hung out. I 'm sure I touched the third day when they called me, which was Thursday morning.

I was in the arraignment part of court. When my case was called, I went back from the courtroom, pass the judge's bench, into a small room with a cage. In back of the cage there's cells where they hold the prisoners, I asked the court officer for my prisoners, they came out. Two sat down on this wooden bench, the one that I took to the hospital stood in front of me. He was still high from the two nights before. I was standing at the time, my back facing the other two; I'm tired and probably off guard. All of a sudden this guy in front pushes me, I go back and down, my neck hits the bench, the two sitting down, hold my shoulders down, the guy in front is on top of me going for my gun. Now the uniform I'm wearing, I'm wearing this leather jacket, which like a rookie I had it tapered, you know you want to look good. I felt like I was in a straight jacket, I yelled to the guard who was on the opposite side of the cage I was in," he's going for my gun", the two behind me let go. I shove the guy on top off of me, now I'm on top of this guy, the one that had his hands on my weapon, I know I'm awake now, I grab my blackjack and about the hit him, I graduated from Billy to Blackjack, the door opens, that's the door I walked in from the court room, I turn around, it's one of the A.D.A.'s, he looks, probably what's taken so long, he sees what's going on, he darts out, after I gain control of the situation, I bring them out, I'm loaded with dust, the court room must have been cleared, because there was no one there. The only thing I saw were court officers all around with guns. The judge asks me if I was okay and if I wanted to re-arrest them. Again, I was so tired, didn't think of going sick, even if I did, I don't think I would have because of being on probation, so I said no.

When I got back to the precinct, I was standing in front of the desk with my overtime slip,.another officer says," hey did you hear about the cop who was jumped in court", I said yea, that was me", he said nothing, just walk away,.on the brighter side, I didn't believe how fast news travels

Till just a couple of years ago I always wondered why the court officer in the cage didn't help me, till this day I could only think, of maybe he had a buzzer, buzzed for help, and again maybe not. Maybe the A.D.A. saw what was happening and calls for assistance. After having more time I the job, I had other cops stand there and do nothing. I have three herniated disk behind my neck, who knows it could have been from that. From that day on all my uniforms I wore were very loose, very, very loose. I was doing a day tour with my partner, the one from the Correction Department. We had a foot post on Coney Island Avenue, when we hear officer needs assistance, some blocks from us. So like young rookies we commandeered a City Bus and head for the location. Hey sorry you missed your stops. Everything's okay, bad call, free ride, plus made your day. They, the passengers would have had a boring night, if they just went to their stop and home. Makes for dinner conversation, hahaha. Maybe even sex.

61PRECINCT & MID TOWN
NORTH PRECINCT

When I got back to the precinct, I was standing In front of the desk with my overtime slip, another officer says," hey did you hear about the cop who was jumped In court", I said yea, that was me", he said nothing, he just walk away. On the brighter side, I didn't believe how fast news travels.

Another time the sergeant and one of the detectives and me are going for a guy that was either wanted for murder or attempted murder. We were going into this building, they tell me to wait here, outside of the building. The guy we want is in a third floor apartment, stay here in case in comes down the fire escape. Still a rookie, I'm waiting, when someone sticks their head out of the second floor window, and I tell him to get back inside. so I'm ready, to make a long story short, they gave me the wrong floor and apartment, I'm under the front fire escape, In front of the building. This guy from the second floor, the one that looked out the second floor window, he shimmies down a sheet, from the side of the building. They gave me the wrong floor, wrong apartment. I could have been killed if he wanted to. When we get back into the car, I knew they felt like shit, so I started to laugh, they looked at me, I said no one got hurt, we'll get him another time. All's well that ends well, another end of tour, we signed out, good job. Again signed out, going home.

We made a collar, with these kids, at that time the big rage were mopeds, two wheel big bikes with motors, you didn't need a license to operate them. These kids, in their teens, decided they wanted new mopeds. It was a Sunday. So they broke a showroom window, where they were selling them and decided to take some. I took the collar; one kid that I locked up was politically connected. We went to arraignment, his lawyer was there. I knew his father was a somebody, the way the lawyer talked to the judge. I wasn't called back to court after that first time, so I figured it was taken care of. Hey lose some win some and learning.

I had a rape collar, where this guy, raped his Aunt while he was visiting her. They were drinking, one thing lead to another and he raped her, then he stole her television set. We grabbed him from a description, with the T V. He was walking down one on the avenues. Description, male white carrying a big T.V.

We bought him back to the location, she said that's him. I arrested him, everyone thought it was bogus, you know drinking and it turned into sex. But every time we had to go to court, and I mean quite a few times. I'd show up and she was there, and I'm talking five or more times in court. I don't know why it was in this part of the court so long, but she was there.

I think it might have been the last show-up for court for me. I'm about to leave for court. The Anti Crime sergeant comes to me, he wants me to change into plain clothes, go with one of the other Anti crime cops, and do a drug buy, I had this rape case, I told him, If I don't show-up, this guy would walk, and If this complaint was that persistent, for her to be In court every time she had to. I believe this guy did It. Sorry can't do. He looked and walked away. Doing undercover buys led to the gold shield faster, If I had to do it over, I'd do the same. Met him years later, I saw him come into the 77 Precinct; he looked at me I looked at him and walked away.

For us to go back to court so many times, I had a hunch this kid and his lawyer were again connected, to someone political, or his family knew someone in the area. The area I arrested him in, there were lot of cops, retired cop and firemen, who lived in that area, only a hunch. On that arrest, two veteran police officers said I should put in for a medal, I passed it up.

It was a midnight tour and I was the sergeant's driver. I think if I remember, only two cars were working that night. We came into the precinct, for the reliefs of the T.S. (telephone switchboard) and the desk relief. The first call I received, the person on the phone said, "There's a woman screaming for help, at a certain location, near a bar." I put it over the air, no units available, the second call, same location, "there's a woman being attacked", again I put it over the air, no units available. A radio car from the 60 pct, said they would respond. Usually something like this a car from a neighboring precinct would take the job or central would ask for one. They were our neighboring precinct, third call, "there's a woman dead in an alley." When the sergeant and I arrived, there was a woman in the rear alley of the bar, her pants down and her throat had been slit.

We found out she walked outside with a guy from the bar, they got a description, the detectives picked him up, he tried to rape her, she fought, so he cut her throat, we found out later It was the brother of one of the cops who worked at the precinct. Years later I was told that the same cop, whose brother killed that woman was locked up for breaking Into police officers lockers at the precinct, he was stealing their guns and selling them on the street. Bad guys don't wear black hats, same as good guys don't wear white hats. Trying to tell the players.

There was this perp, who was working the precincts. his M.O. Or motes apprentice was robberies of Carvel stores. He would enter holding a gun and he wore a band aid across his nose, he was dubbed the band aid bandit. Most precincts In the Brooklyn south area had Carvel stores and were after him too. Sometimes he would hit the same store twice, so you knew he had balls or just stupid. The 69 precinct collared him,.I was notified by the desk officer, to go down to the 69 precinct and stand in a lineup. He was around my height a little taller, brown to sandy brown hair, built similar. When I got to the 69, they briefed me what was going on. Still a rookie I was a little nervous. The complaints picked the same guy, which the 69 picked up.

About a week later, I'm driving home after a four by twelve. I usually take the same route, down avenue S in Brooklyn. Usually on that drive, I see an R.M.P., doubled parked on avenue S and west 9th street, most of the nights. This time that I was driving home, no police car. I'm going to make my left onto west 10th street where I lived at the time. I looked to the right and saw a doubled parked car, with its hood open, two guys near a parked car, its hood opened. I said to myself, a little late to be working on a car. So I went around the block. I passed these two guys; they were taking a battery from the parked car, to theirs. Who do I recognize as one of the perps, but the guy that was picked out of the lineup, the band aid bandit. Here's what ran through my mind in split second. It's late, no radio, draw my gun hold them start yelling for help, what if no one pays attention. So I passed them, took a description of the car and perps, went home. Called the 69th precinct detective squad, the detective that had the case for the carvel robberies would be in, in the morning. I called the next day spoke to him, I told him, I was In your lineup just last week, told him what I saw, gave him what details I had, I said you're trying to tell me this guy did many armed robberies and he's on the street already, ... dumb rookie that's me telling myself.

I remember doing a day tour, when we get a 1085, police officer needs back-up. Sheepshead bay, the Knapp street area. It was at a wedding hall. When we walked into the lobby of the wedding hall, there's a total, [both sides], wedding fight going on. We went in with all the other backups and started to break up what was going on. I saw one girl in a gown jump on the back of a police officer, when I saw this, a seasoned cop grabbed her by the hair and yanked the shit out of her, she must have been tossed about ten feet, she probably though she was untouchable, because she had a gown on, rude awakening, I wasn't just standing there, but totally aware. After the situation was under control. This is how It started, someone from the grooms side, said something to someone from the bride's side, push came to shove. Not a happy day. Open my eyes about the opposite sex. Wonder if they did the envelopes first?

I was driving with my partner at the time. The young cop who was the C.O., and same time on the job as me. We were doing a four by twelve. We decided to go out of sector, to Sheepshead Bay, It was the weekend. we were driving along the water where all the restaurants were, the streets are very narrow, enough for one or two cars, and along the restaurant side of the street, there were all cars doubled parked, which made it even harder to pass. We drove by, saw match books in the windows of most of the cars, I heard about the match books from the time of the Knapp Commission. This meant that there was no more parking spots in the area and the match books would tell you what restaurant the customer was in, and no summons were given, and here it was. So as rookies' we decided to bang all the cars, not because of the match books.

The ones that we banged, because the people that were taken care of the cars, didn't give a shit how difficult it was for the cars that had to pass and the crowds of people trying to walk by at this time of night. We left, after we did our good deed and returned to our own sector.

We get a call on the radio to meet a certain sector at a specific location. I'm the recorder; we pulled alongside the sector car that made the call. There's an old timer and a younger cop, the younger cop had time on the job. I recognized them; they were hooked up as partners. the old timer says who's Cimino, I said that's me, he tells me you gave out summons in my sector, he tells me, "stay out of his sector." I looked at him, I point to my shield, I said "see this, It says city of New York," and we left.

I'm sure after that incident; they pulled us out of the car, and gave us both foot posts on Coney Island Avenue. We were on day tours. So we banged all the cars on Coney Island Ave for meters, unregistered and uninspected vehicles. That area was a commercial and residential area, we stayed there for a couple of days then they put us back in our sector. At that time it was unusual for rookies to have a sector.

I was doing a late tour when a burglary in progress came over the air, on Ocean Avenue, around the Sheepshead Bay section, the perp was on the roof of one of the supermarkets. When we get there with other sectors, we search around the building and find a rope going from roof to the ground. Some of the guys go to the roof and grabbed this kid, early teens, dressed all in black, with cap trying to go through the roof of the supermarket. He was bagged for attempted burglary. The most important thing that the kid failed to realize was that the roof of the supermarket was one story high. the buildings around the supermarket, were high rise buildings, one of the tenants who lived on the upper floor of their building, spotted him through their window, and called it in. not his calling. Sorry ninja, no invisibility.

I had a foot post on a four by twelve, when I met this complainant at her house, an elderly women living by herself, and very upset. She tells me her story. Every time she's asleep, around two or three in the morning the phone would ring and there were kids on the phone harassing her. This was happening for months, and she was crying, as she was talking to me. So I take a report and referred it to the detectives. I bring the report up myself and I said how about we do a wire tap. They looked at me as if I was crazy. They told me it was a big thing to do a tap. I think I was being blown off, and that rookie shit look on their face. This word shit comes up a lot, hmmm, wondering, could be part of my limited vocabulary.

My ex wife has an aunt in New Jersey, so one time I was visiting. I'm talking to her husband about this woman and the phone calls, and how I wanted to get a wire tap and the way I was blown off by the detectives. He comes out and tells me, which I didn't know. I'm and Investigator for the phone company. He tells me, Al, get me a detectives name and a 61 number and I'll set up the tap. When I get back to the precinct, I go up to the squad, I tell them, I have a wire tap set up, he said alls he needs, Is a Dicks name and a 61 number, I saw the expression on their faces. They said, ok, we'll go out and talk to this woman.

I left It in there hands. Nice to have friends in high and low places. This guy from the phone company who lived In New Jersey, nicest guy you want to meet, sometime later, after retirement he passed away of cancer. This guy knew how to live. He and his wife, my ex-wife's aunt made a great couple, two of a kind. Till today even after my divorce we still keep in touch. Bill and Ann.

We locked up this kid for G.L.A., [grand larceny auto.] we have him in the car and we're taking him to Central booking. I'm in the recorders seat, I turn and I'm looking at him. I tell him, you know, you're a good looking guy, your young, why don't you just get yourself a job and make some money. He says where at, what Mc Donald's. I'm making three hundred for every car I steal. Now what? Intelligence report.

I was doing an eight by four day tour. I was going to Central Booking. I passed this social club, when I thought I saw, a girl being dragged in, and she was fighting to be free. I told my partner to stop the car, by the way we were going to Central Booking to pick up police officer to give him a lift back to the precinct, so I told the driver to stop. I jumped out went into the social club, ask and look

Around saw nothing wrong, I made sure everything was ok. I went out and my partner was still sitting In the R.M.P., no help from him, not even a question asked, sure I told him I think there's a problem there, this was the second time I worked with this guy and both times when I thought there was trouble, he sat In the car. the second time he was driving and I was the recorder going down Coney Island avenue, when we passed a bank and I saw some guy coming off the roof of the bank, I told him to stop the car, I got out, had this guy, It was like an alley against the wall.

I questioned him, big kid, let him go. The driver, he was from, I think a north precinct or a precinct where he did his time, sat in the car again said nothing that was the last time I rode with him. Me personally I think he had It with the job and just buying his time, myself new and gun-ho, I knew he wasn't with It anymore, hey, live and learn. As the years went on in the job, met other Police Officer who just wore the uniform, they were called empty suits.

MIDTOWN NORH PRECINCT:

TRANSFERRED

I was transferred to the Midtown North precinct. [M.T.N.] 54 streets between 8th and 9th avenues. This precinct was from the old school precinct, the old telephone switch board, and the cells right on the first floor. It felt like you were walking into the past. The real hustle and bustle of a precinct, nice feeling.

The first three days were orientation. About prostitution and making sure you don't fall in love with any of the Prose's. I thought they were kidding but when you saw some of the hookers, I understood, In other words, falling In love with a prostitute can get you into a lot of trouble and some of them were lookers. The precinct was mainly known for pimps and loads of Pros.

Every so often they would make a sweep, load up the paddy wagons with the prostitutes and book them. When they came in the cops knew them on a first name basis and so did the girls or transvestites. The pimps or their lawyers would meet them in court; pay the fine, than back on the street again. the police offices knew them, so they, the Pros. would decide, well It's your turn to be locked up, I was there last week, or whose turn is it now to get locked up.

Most of the precinct was foot patrol, the one thing they told you while on foot, in certain areas, was to watch out or be careful, because they threw things off the roofs. Such as bowling balls, toilet bowels etc, so in that area it was good to walk in the street next to the parked cars. When you did get a sector and you had a heavy call, especially on weekends the traffic was so heavy that sometimes most of the time, you took the sidewalks, If a call was on your beat, the footman would tell central he'd take the job, unless It was a heavy job than he would back—up the sector.

I remember on a day tour, a lieutenant on the desk, Again rumor, he was under Investigation from I.A.D. He told me to go with these guys, they had a court order to seal up a building with sheet metal, and make sure there was no trouble. When I got there, they already started sealing up the doors and windows. Nobody mentioned that there were squatters in the building. But they had a court order. I told them you're not sealing up this building, what are you people nuts there's people in this building. We went back to the precinct; I told the lieutenant, what the situation was. The people with the court order left, they went back to court. Didn't get an ending result. No common sense

We heard a radio run, burglary in progress, I don't remember what block, when you were on foot, again, If It was In your post, you would take the job and free the R.M.P. When I get there, it was a four or five story building. The police officers were on the roof, all veterans, when I got to the roof. A new sight for new eyes. I saw two seasoned cops dangling this known burglar off the roof by his feet, they looked at me, and say, "Cimino, should we drop him", I said," naa, I don't think It's a good idea", still, new guy on the block. they brought him back up, for some reason; I knew they would have let him go, if I said," yea drop him". Just for being a pain in the ass. wasn't the only time I had to make a call like that. I'm glad I took them serious.

Another big thing was the fixers in this precinct, either guarding glass on Fifth Avenue, or, having a fixer at the Embassy buildings. With the glass, you had to stand In front of a store all night, on late tours and make sure no one broke the windows. That was because of the Fifth Avenue Commerce Association in this area, they ran the precinct; and they had a lot of political power.

The other big thing was the Diplomats and their Diplomatic Immunity status. If you had an Incident with a diplomat, you'd have to call a sergeant to the scene.

I was walking my beat, around Fifth Avenue near ST. Patrick's Cathedral, when I run into a cab dispute. the cab driver and the passengers, one a great looking female and a well dressed good looking older man, the dispute was over, I think It was, a buck and a half fare. He wasn't going to pay the fare. The traffic was backed up; it was taking to long, so they decided to get out of the cab, and decided to walk. The cabbie threw down the meter; it was for a dollar and a half. Now he doesn't want to pay. I'm trying to reason with this guy. We're going back and forth. When all of a sudden, he shows me a card and declares Diplomatic Immunity. I didn't believe it, I thought it was a joke, I turned around, I say to the girl, "you're going out with this guy, and you're not embarrassed, you got to be kidding." He must have regained his senses, I saw a smile on his face, he says to me, "I'll give you the money and you pay him, "I say "you give the girl the money and let her pay." that's what he did, diplomatic incident settled, and unbelievable. This would be my first and not the last.

Another time, they had me guarding some Russian ship, as a fixer, that's because I didn't have the wire in my hat that holds the top of the hat stiff. The sergeant that gave it to me, the fixer, you didn't mind, because that was his mentality. This is what happened. We were walking our post, passing stores when I saw him coming up on us from his reflection in the stores glass, he's sneaking up on us, then he yells got-cha, see you were too busy talking and you didn't even see me, Get my meaning. Hey simple. They warned me about him. He was the guy that told me about no wire. I have to learn to keep my mouth shut. Yea right.

With that fixer West Side Highway, I mean it was freezing, and every hour a scratch. After a few scratches, I said to myself fuck this, do what you have to do, I went into the pier building that was behind me, I stayed there, and no one said anything to me. Colder than a Witches Tit, Always wanted to say that, never had a place for it until that day. Ah poetry.

I'm walking 5th avenue with a partner, each tour was almost a different police officer for a partner, and we get a call to Cartiers, the jewelry store, a very prestigious store. When we get there, the clerk says, some guy came in and was going to pass a counterfeit check, from a well known bank, he had Irving trust checks. This guy is dressed in a sweater and slacks. When we go outside, we spot him going up Fifth Avenue, we grabbed him and bring him back, and yes that's him. This is how it went down.

He comes into the store with a woman, she's all dressed up. They select a $15,000 ring, and say, he'll be back with a cashier's check, from Irving trust. This is around Friday mid morning. When he returns, it was just around three o'clock that afternoon, this time by himself. He probably thought the clerk would be looking for the fast sale, the banks are closed, he won't check on the check because it was a certified check. The guy looked a little nervous, so they tell him to wait. I guess the clerk and his boss do a check on the check, there's probably a phone number they could call after hours to verify if the check is good. I think the check was a cashier's check. They find out the check is bogus or counterfeit. They called the police. When the clerk gets back to the counter, they tell him he has to wait; it'll take a few minutes. He starts to get nervous and leaves. We were just steps away from the store when the call was made to the police. My partner took the collar. The girl wasn't there the second visit, she was just their for window dressing. This guy was around 50 years of age, still doing drugs, he was a small times rackets guy, low level organize crime guy. Because of the counterfeit check, and he had more checks with the name and logo of the bank when we tossed him. The F.B.I. had to be notified. It was good that the clerk was on the ball.

When you're a rookie the veterans could get over on you, this guy that I was working with wasn't a collar guy, but he took It, because he knew it was a good arrest. Sometimes I still don't learn it'll happen again, and It did a few times, nice guys do finish last, but I can look myself In the mirror and smile, or say Sap.

I used to get foot posts on day tours, a lot. When I had them, especially on Broadway, the big thing, was to give out summons.

So when I walked the post, I tried to read the no parking signs, I couldn't understand what the fuck they meant, you couldn't park here from this time to that time under these conditions or that condition. so I said to myself, If I can't understand these signs, how the fuck can a civilian understand what they meant, so I said fuck It, and I didn't give out any summons for the signs. I told one of the sergeants, that I wasn't giving out summons, and I told him why, he looked and said, okay," then give out parking meter summons. Easy to read", will do.

I was on another foot post, when I saw this guy lying on the ground against a building. I asked him his name anything wrong, he was incoherent. So I called for a bus. I rode with the bus to one of the hospitals. Filling out parts of the aided card that I could fill out. When we got to the hospital, they all seemed to know him, for his age I don't know If I put thirty plus or forty plus. To make a long story short he was a regular and alcoholic 19 years of age, blew me away. From there we took him to another location, I think It was called the tank. It was a building where they would dry out, put them back on the street and they would start over again. We should stop meeting like this, I'll see him again.

The fixers; like I mentioned, and the Fifth Avenue Commerce Association had all the pull in the precinct. On a twelve by eight, with some of the stores they had their own private cops, us, N.Y.P.D., standing their watching their windows. The rumor was, if the glass was broken, you had better be, either critical wounded or dead, was the only excuse that was accepted. The other fixer was at the Embassy buildings. It was a two man detail one man in, one man out. The man in, had a key to the back door of the Embassy, I'm saying Embassy or something affiliated with them. He would stay for an hour, then come down and relieve his partner. on a cold winter night this was great, but as usual, we got sloppy and made pigs of ourselves, by drinking there liquor, or leaving the place a mess. So now, no keys, and we had to stay out and freeze our asses off. This was for the few guys who didn't give a fuck about anyone but themselves. Just like the academy, and the duck walk.

27

The other fixer was the travel agencies. What a waste of police manpower. Almost as good as the fixer that was in the 61 precinct, we were guarding the Inspectors tree that he just planted in front of his house to make sure no one destroyed it.

Four by twelve we raided a brothel, or whore house. When we went in through the door, there were all types of people in the waiting area to be serviced. The one person I remembered was, well he looked like a Rabbi, he wore that thing around his neck that looked like a scarf, sitting there meek, and like," oh shit I'm not here", kind of look. They had separate rooms or cubicles, where the girls and their clients would go, very well organized. Hey Organized.

LAID OFF, BUDGET CRISES

B y this time there were rumors about New York City police officers being laid off, on account of the budget shortage. We were in roll call at the time, the delegates were talking to the men about giving up a weeks' pay, not to have cops laid off. The cops that were going to be laid off were sitting there too. There was a big debate yelling, no, fuck, these guys, we're not giving up a weeks' pay, we need the money, that's camaraderie for you. They didn't give a shit. When the time came, Midtown North, that's where I turned in my gun and shield. We were heartbroken.

I was laid off for about two years. I was out of work and I was living in Brooklyn at the time. I was still gun ho. So, the first job interview I went on was at, I think the address was 2 federal plaza or F.B.I headquarters. I figured why not. I have nothing to lose. When I got there, I went to the personnel office told them I was interested in becoming an agent, for some reason, I got an interview with the Director. We talked, he said, you know this job in mostly administrative, or paper work, I nodded; I told him I was a laid off police officer. He asked me how many years did I have on the job, I said a little less than two, he said, I needed five years working as a police officer, and it would have been no problem to transfer over. When I walked out it made me feel good, just to know I got the interview, and that I could have been up in that kind of rank of a job.

One of my neighbors, also a laid off Police officer, real nice guy a Golden Glover, asked me if I wanted a job where he was working. It was at a security firm. He gave me the address, I went down. I didn't have a clue, so I showed up in dungarees and a T shirt. I met one of the owners, name Ron, I introduced myself, then I went into another office, I guess the big boss, Rudy, he was also, I think the main owner, he had connections with the F.B.I. The security firm was named Centurion, I sat down, we talk, great guys, both of them and he hired me.

During that time, I worked with a bunch of great guys, all laid off cops. It was my pleasure to have known them and to have worked with them.

My first job was in Coney Island. Since I was the new guy on the block, I was put in a high rise complex, alone, there was a lot of burglaries, robberies and a lot of toughs, who hung out in the lobby and around the building. My job, was to hang out in the lobby make sure there was no trouble. Sometimes I would take the stairs, walked the floors. I was getting to know who was who in the building. I would tell them to move, or you're making too much noise.

When I got to the building, this first building I worked in, the people that lived there would not even look at me. When they started seeing me there every day and some nights, and after the lobby was cleaned out, they started giving me a look of appreciation, and some came over and said hello. The reason why people in these types of neighborhoods do not talk to the police or any type of authority they're afraid of retaliation, because the bad guys might think you're ratting or giving information. One guy I met was giving information and he was killed, this was in the seven-seven precinct

One day, they hooked me up with a black security guy in uniform, I was in plains clothes. These two toughs, one name Kojack and his friend, I was told about him by one of the guys I made friends with, they were scared of these two guys. They were standing in the lobby, I told them to move, they gave me a hard time. So I attack them, and threw them both up against the wall. The security guard stood there, and did nothing. After that they both left, they said we're coming back. I told the security guard, if you're going to stand there and do nothing, make a phone call, tell the guys I need back-up. He left. I was hoping he would make the call. Maybe five minutes later the boys show up, nine guys with guns, my friends. I told them what went down. So all nine made themselves comfortable in the lobby.

Who comes through the doors, the two I threw out plus this guy that looked like he could lift the building, and looking mean. I walked up to him, he looked behind me, saw the boys sitting and standing in the lobby. He apologized for even showing up, and they left. I had no trouble from them after that. I stayed there another week or so. No one was hanging out in the lobby, nice and clean and I knew word got around. After that incident, the guys told me to hang out in the building they were in. They left the security guard there.

While hanging out with the guys in that building they were in. They found out that a super or one of the supers was doing burglaries. He would enter apartments with pass keys and take stuff. The guys found the stolen stuff in an elevator engine room atop of this building. The building being twenty to twenty six stories up.

Frank and I was doing a late tour, and we staked out the room on top of the building, figuring he would come up and start taking the stuff, it was dark cold and damp. We stayed there all night, no show.

After that job. We had a job at Cartiers, plain clothes. A diamond was on display. If I'm not mistaken it was the diamond that Richard Burton bought for his wife Elizabeth Taylor, one hundred and seven carats. Second time I worked with this laid off police officer, Frank the one from the stakeout at Coney Island, he was from the 9th precinct in Manhattan. I believe we were becoming friends. So we're there, day shift, he comes back to me, hey I think there's a guy on the top floor with a gun. He starts moving I'm right behind him. We take the stairs. He spots him,

31

I go up to the guy, now you got to remember, that Cartiers is a major jewelry firm, with very important clients, if you say, or do something wrong you're out, and possible the firm. So I went up to this guy, not eyeing him, checking him out, belt clothes, I went back to Frank I said I don't think so. Plus he looked like he was there to buy. We went back to our positions.

Then, from there, I did a personal body guard job for Cartier's. It was my day off. I was painting my apartment, when the phone rang. It was my boss, he says, Al, I have a job if you want it, he tells me, I would have to go to Cartier's, there will be a limousine waiting for me. You're going to take two females and about three million dollars in antique jewelry to the airport. All you have to do is make sure it gets there, they're going to France. I said "okay, no problem." When I get there, I met another guy, Joe; he's a, dapper sweet talker, good guy.

First we went to the top floor of Cartier's. We see the girls. We go downstairs. He jumps in the back of the limo with the two girls, or two executives, I sat in the front seat with the driver, always checking my mirrors . . . we get to the airport, no problems. Because of Cartier's and the influence that Cartiers has, the customs agents came to them. Again, no problem, we get seated in the first class lounge. I'm always standing, looking around,.everyone in there are having drinks and eating. We waited until they get on the plane, and we leave . . . nice experience. It was like the movie "The Body Guard" with Kevin Costner; too bad we did it first.

When I was still at Cartier's, 'I'll tell you how observant I am, when it comes to females. There was this girl behind the counter she was selling jewelry, very pretty, I used to see her every time I worked, talked a little, smiled at each other, again I didn't have a clue that she liked me. So one day, the guys comes over to me and say, hey Al, do you know that girl wants to go out with you, I said you're kidding, no, and she's the daughter of an assemblyman, my response, I can't, I going out with someone already, they say." hey Al she's the daughter of an assemblyman,""no I can't." Stupid me, for being and having ethics and morals, was to find out much later, my wife didn't have any.

Another nice job we had. We did a job for Christies, the auction house; I think there main branch is located in London. From what I heard they bought two floors in a Park Avenue hotel. They were setting up the floor and they must have had three to five hundred million dollars worth of art work there, and they wanted to make sure it stayed. They had this art worked stored in two rooms, next door to each other. The boss from our firm was there with the guys.

I'm looking around, and I said I didn't like the idea, not knowing, or seeing the other team, who were going to be in the other room. So one of the big bosses of Christie's, said no problem, we'll break down the wall and make it one big room. Then I asked, if all the art work would fit in one room. That's what they did, they put all in one room, it was a bit tight, but cozy, again no problem. Christies treated us very well.

We did the security, when the place was finished and they had one huge auction. For two days we were in this huge room with the paintings hung on the walls and wherever the rest were.

I called the first day of the auction, new money, these people or prospective buyers came in tuxes and gowns. We were in plain clothes. The time they finished eating and drinking, when they left, some were sloshed or tanked to the gills, some barely walking straight.

Again I'm with one of the owners. Some guy comes over to us and starts giving us orders. This is what he wants; this is what you're going to do. I look at him, I said, who are you, I don't remember either the C.F.O. or an accountant, some wannabe big wig. I tell him, "look, you take care of the numbers; we'll take care of the security." He looked like he was pissed, he walked away. I apologized to Ron, the owner. He said Al, no problem; take care of the security, that's your job.

The second day of the auction, this time I called it, old money, these people wore jeans, flannel shirts, casual dress, very polite, friendly saw us, said hello, no problem, nice experience

You can take a horse to water but you can't make him drink, unless it's free . . .

Another job; we were supposed to go under cover for the Long Island Railroad. There was a scam going on with the people that were taking the tickets from the passengers on the trains. It never materialized because.

Newspapers headlines:

TWO THOUSAND POLICE

OFFICERS

TO BE REHIRED:

I received my assignment, 63—precinct. I hooked up with another laid off cop.

The generous thing the City did for us was that we had the option to buy back the time that we were laid off. All we had to do was put back the two years pension money that was missing from the time of being laid off. In a heartbeat, they took it out of my pay until it was paid, so in reality I only served eighteen years on the job. Not bad, for a guy who never liked work, and when you love a job it's not work, and did I love being a police officer.

I remember we were eating in this dinner on a late tour, sitting in a booth, when this drunk takes a seat next to my partner and starts talking, me personally I can't stand drunks because you never know what's coming up next, well what was coming up, he pushed my partner in the booth and stands up, I get up, hit him in the chest he goes flying through the entrance door that lead through the bathroom door entrances. I jumped on him. He tells me, you can't do this. I say watch me, you're under arrest.

We take him to the precinct, I give him a dis-con-summons, he tells me his father's on the job. I said" You should have thought of that before this happened."We released him. We go back on patrol. We get a ten-two, and we go back to the house, the 124 room guy.

35

[He's the person that types up all the paperwork,] a civilian, tells me, the kids father called, who happened to be a detective first grade, if he can do anything about the summons. The 124 guy was always a little too cocky; he decides to take care of it himself, before telling me. I caught between a rock and a hard place. I give him a look, now he knows he over stepped his bounds, I walk out. The next night we're on meal, same diner, some big guy walks in with the guy we took in for the dis-con-summon the night before. I figure trouble, the big guy tells the kid ok, tell them,

He says, he never done this before and apologizes. The big guy says he's his father, tells me he's a detective 1st grade, he's sorry for what his son did. We shook hands. He gave me his card. Says if there's anything I can do, just call me. They leave. In a way, I was glad the summons was taken care of, but I didn't like the way it was done. As we were about to pay for the check, the clerk said, it was taken care of. Big guy, gentleman.

The captain at the 63 precinct was a gentleman, not a pushover. He called me into his office one day, and he said some of your friends were concerned, because they thought something was wrong. I said, yea I'm getting married, and I'm a little nervous. He looked at me, said, most marriages get into trouble because of money. I said no not mine, he smiled, only time someone was concerned about me, felt good, felt odd, but good.

One day he asked me to drive him and I think someone else, came along too. We drove where the Brooklyn court buildings were. It was raining. I'm driving down Flatbush Avenue. He started to become a front seat driver, it's raining, watch this, watch that. I pulled the car over to the curb, on Flatbush, stop the car. I said okay, here, either you drive or I drive. He looked at me, smiled, okay, I drove. We're driving, still on Flatbush Avenue, we pass a small store, and he said look, Karate University, and chuckles, not too much. Good, dry sense of humor. The store was a little bigger than a bread box. University.

I met him a few years later at the 77 precinct. He was promoted to Deputy Inspector. Strange.

There was this coffee shop at the junction on Flatbush Avenue, where I use to have coffee. It was a mom and pop place. The owner, a grouchy Greek guy, he never had a smile on his face, always complaining. I got the feeling he never wanted me there, his wife totally the opposite. I think the cook was his brother-in-law. I went there because he made me pay for what I ate. I felt like I didn't owe him anything. As I continued to eat, we talked, not much, his wife always pleasant.

Sometime later, I was doing a midnight tour. I went in for coffee, they all were very nervous, I said, what's wrong. He said, he had a guy lock of for robbery, and his friends came in and threaten him. He had to go to court in the morning. So he asked me if I could go with him, I said let me think about it.

Now, I know, after a late tour how I feel, like, tired and I want to go home to sleep. When the tour ended, the thing I asked myself, what's the easy thing to do? It would be for me to forget about it and go home. So I went to the coffee shop, they were extremely happy to see me; the Greek must have shown a tooth. We hung out for awhile, and then left for court.

We go into the court room, sit down and wait, there are people behind us to the right, and two more guys sit down in the row behind ours. Now I see him cringe. I look behind, they're looking at him. His name was George,.than they look at me. When the judge came in, we stood, I stretched, turned a little, I showed them my gun. They left. He gets called. The judge, the lawyers talked. George talks, we all leave. He thinks he got railroaded. What can I say . . . I take him back to the coffee shop, it's about 5:30pm; drop him off,.go home. Sleep . . . another late tour. Man, did I hate late tours.

I went to see him, still paid for the coffee, much better attitude. Through the years every once in a while, I took a free cup.

I met him again, when I transferred to the 77 precinct. He sold the coffee shop at the Junction and opened one in the 78 precinct. That's where one of their son's, I think his name was Joseph, worked and the first time I met him. I walked into this coffee shop, it was out of precinct. Every once in a while you wanted to get out of the precinct for meal ... who's there, the whole family, old home week, big greeting, we sit down, ordered. I didn't know it was his coffee shop.

This time, he's cleaning the windows, again late tour, one of the window breaks, a piece of glass hits him on the head, big gash, he's bleeding, the families scared and they look at me, I ask my partner, OK, we take him to the hospital. That might have been the last time I saw him. His son that was working there was on the list for the police department. Don't know if he got on or not, wished him luck.

There was this handout on Utica Avenue where they were selling and doing drugs. Big crowd of teenagers hanging out on the sidewalk and in front of the store. They were blocking people from walking on the sidewalk. My partner the other laid off police officer and I were breaking there balls, until we found out who was who, and who the wise guys were.

I remember as I was talking to some of them, I turn and see my partner in the street; he grabbed one guy by the hair, who wasn't listening. We brought him back to the house, gave him a dis-con-summons. We went there every chance we had, to break up the crowd and disturb there routine, tried to put fear of god in the ones who were selling the drugs and doing the buying.

We were doing a four by twelve. We're walking to the radio car, when the girl on the T.S., telephone switchboard, comes out; she tells me that she just got a phone call, no name. Tell Cimino to stay away from Utica Avenue or we're going to get him, boy was I was pissed. I went back into the house told the lieutenant about the phone call. He tells me don't worry about it, you're gonna get many more as the time goes on with the job. I found out later on in my career, that people should have been notified and a report should have been made. When you're new, you don't know. Well I'm still pissed. I got into the radio car told my partner about the call. My partner drove; I'm doing a lot of thinking and calming down.

We were driving down Flatbush Avenue, this guy was double parked in front of a parking space, I told my partner to stop, I gave him a summons, told him to park it, I knew I talked nasty to him,

I shouldn't have, my problem' is not with him. We drove away. I tell my partner to go back to where we gave the summons. I went back to see the person that I gave the summon to. I got out of the car went into the store, I told the guy what happened, and apologized, he said, thanks, don't worry about it. I always tried not to let my personal feelings or my angry be given to a person that should not get it. I never like that, it puts more fuel to the fire, but to each his or her own.

I had a suspicion who made the phone call to the precinct. So we went looking for him. You know, back and forth between jobs. I figured, it was around mid tour, we spotted him on one on the avenues, he spots us, and he starts running. My partner stopped the car; I jumped out and started chasing him. This was not the first time that I jump out of the R.M.P., started a foot chase. We're running through alleys, over fences. I didn't realize my partner called in a 10-13, officer needs assistance, sometimes I forget to let my partner in on what I'm going to do and just go. I chased him through this apartment house corridor, it was dead end. The big tough guy starts crying. I cuff him, I go outside, I see the sergeant all these radio cars, I didn't even think of taking a radio. It felt good to know you had backup. In the years to come, I'll have different stories about backups. We took him in again discon-summons. Make a long story short, broke up that old gang of mine. We'd passed by, a lot more respect. No crowd.

This same lieutenant, I remember, everyone was afraid of him, he was a hard nose. So one day, a day tour, I heard that two of the P.B.A. delegates were taken out of the car and put on a foot post, by him. I'm sure I ask the two delegates if they wanted me to see what I can do to get them back into their car,.they looked dumb founded. So I told they lieutenant if I can talk to him in Private, I told him I didn't believe you would do such a thing, about taking them out of their car, for such a small thing. Make a long story short the next day they were put back into their sector, when they, saw me, one was P.B.A. delegates they looked at me and just walked away.

My partner and I were sent to the 60 pct for a detail, Coney Island area. We took a precinct R.M.P. When we got there, we went into the Muster room. A boss came in and told us and the other cops what had happened that day. It seems that there was a shooting; I think it might have been some plain clothes police officers from anti crime, a Hispanic was killed. The precinct got a phone call that some cars were going to pass the precinct and fire shotguns at the cops. When we got there I noticed the windows of the precinct had their metal shutters down, made sense. So our job was, and the other cops, to stand in front of the precinct, OK, some cars were going to pass by and start shooting at the precinct. I was going to say something to the boss, but I didn't, and stand in front

We hung around inside for a while, then went out. I realized how stupid it was, when I saw them moving the R.M.P.'s [auto's] out from in front of the precinct, because, if they did come, they didn't want the cars to be damaged. Cars would have been a perfect cover for us, I'm still looking around

What they did is, they put the cops behind barriers, and you know the wood horses with a board going across, may be six to eight inches wide. I told my partner, fuck this. We took our precinct R.M.P. that we came down in, across the street from the precinct there was a housing project and right in front of the building facing the cops and wooden horses and the precinct doors was the housing project's parking lot. I took the R.M.P., went into the parking lot, put it facing the cops, who were standing outside. I told my partner, fuck it, if they come, will ram the shit out of them. Anybody for an Inspector's funeral? They never showed. Sometimes it just doesn't make sense.

A small bit of information. The way rules and laws can be changed by popular demand. There was this one area in Bergen Beach, where if you parallel parked there weren't enough parking spaces for the residents, so they started to park perpendicular to the curb. Since it was a well to do area and the people in that area probably had pull no summons were given, and after that it was no problem parking that way. Me personally I saw no problem, with that kind of parking. Because across from the houses, there was like an open field, or marsh land. So they weren't blocking any other traffic. You look at something if there's a better way of doing it and nobody is being hurt or bothered, go for it.

Just a little bit of talk or a way of thinking. There was this rookie in the precinct that they labeled a coward. Some of the guys came over to me and said watch-out when you work with him, again he's a coward, never liked that word coward. I rode with him once or twice, he looked at me, like he was thinking, you heard about me and what they're saying. I never said a word, I think I made him comfortable and we had a good tour.

I met up with him years later. He was working in a Brooklyn North precinct. He was handing out the radios at the time and I was flying there for the day. When I saw him, he gave me that same look, like his past caught up with him again. I think I saw the fear in his eyes, like I was going to tell everyone. The only thing I did was say hi, and walked away. My thing is, if there were ten rules in life and you only could go up to number three or four than that's how far you go in life, you were never taught anything else, this is where you are in the Book of Life, there's no thing as a coward. Just didn't learn how to . . . Life is hard enough without giving some one more baggage.

When I first got to the 61 precinct, don't remember if it was the first day first week. One of the veteran cops says, hey rookie, with a snarl, I turn, and say I don't like being called that. This was the same cop that told me later on not to give summons out in his sector.

Another veteran, from a high crime precinct, big heavy set cop, says you want to see the enforcer; sure, he reaches into his front pants and takes out this single barreled shot gun, the one with the hand grip. Like wow, full of surprises. Academy, "remember make sure you go for the groin, and check for weapons."

63PCT TRANSFER TO 77PCT

A small tad-bit of information, I had a foot post one day in the 63 precinct. I ran into an elderly lady, I would say in her sixties to early seventies. We started talking; she was telling me about the drug dealings in the area, she tells me she is working with the F.B.I. I thought she was, you know, maybe a little off. I took her name down. So when I get back to the precinct, I say why not, so I call your local F.B.I. office. I spoke to an agent. I give him the story and her name. He tells me to hold on. He comes back, says they know her and every once in a while she gives them some useful information. Hum you don't say. That's an eye opener. The eyes and ears of the street, collecting social security.

I always worked in the Brooklyn south area, except for certain details. Every time I made a collar and went to central booking. I used to see these Brooklyn north cops walk in. they had a certain air about them, and I'm talking from a good point of view. Unless it was a north cop transfer to a south precinct, they were more self confident, right in the moment. They looked like they had more control of a situation. Something that I didn't feel or see with a Brooklyn South cop, except for the cops I knew that came from the North precincts'. This I knew was in the back of my mind for some time, without me realizing it; it would come to my front soon. I'm not knocking the Brooklyn South cops, met and worked with a hell of a lot of good cops there, but for me maybe I needed more. I had a few good and knowledgeable partners there.

I went on this detail. There was a demonstration in front of the Brooklyn Public Library. A police officer, tried to restrain a person with his night stick, and he died. The tension in the street was on high. When I got there I asked what precinct was this. They said the 77 precinct. For some reason internally I heard my name being called, I felt like it was a calling; like I belonged in this area. I didn't know where the precinct was located. This at around the time I got married. I moved in my wife's uncle's house on Fulton Avenue and Vanderbilt Avenue. A very short time later I put in for a transfer. You can pick a first choice, second and third choice of precincts that you wanted to transfer to. I only picked the 77 precinct. About a month later, I was transfer.

The precinct was located on Utica Avenue and Bergen Street. I lived one block out of the boundary of the 77 precinct. This is where I became a cop, and I guess grew up, and found out what the job was really about, the good the bad and the ugly.

I remembered walking into the precinct. The first thing that came to my mind was that this precinct is dirty, first major gut feeling. I remember being in the lunch room, I guess that's where I took my first stand I don't know why. I'm not usually like that. I said if anyone is doing anything wrong; don't work with me because I'm straight. And I walked out and went into the bathroom. Another cop came in; he introduced himself, told me his partner had been killed here. I didn't know what to say, so I just listened to him talk. This guy did ten years as a police officer and then transferred to the fire department.

They gave me a foot post. At this time I didn't know how bad the area was. In time I found out. I'm walking down one of the blocks, Bergen street, I turn right onto Rochester avenue, I walk maybe five hundred feet, some guy walks up to me, he says he's the numbers man in this area. Like, what the fuck, I give him a look. He realizes I'm a new guy on the block, and I didn't know about the program, as of yet, he just cowardly walks away. I guess my first awaking. Just by the way the guys looked at me, I knew they didn't trust me, I knew that it was more than what meets the eye. Something deeper than what I knew about, because I still had the rookie feelings that all cops were brothers and corruption was the furthest thing from my mind, big and small. I'm getting ahead of myself, most of the people and the stores that I went into thought that all cops were corrupt; I believe I started changing some of their attitudes as time went by.

There was a burglary on my post, in progress. I saw some guy going up a fire escape into a back window, broad daylight, like there's a set time for a burglary. I get there, so does Anti Crime. They took the collar. But one of the Anti Crime guys he looked familiar. I remembered I met him from years ago in the 61 precinct. We got a call to his house, possibly break in, he was there, that's where he lived. He had a police radio. The reason why he had a police radio, was because in doing his job, he was threatened by some drug dealers, someone or people were out to kill him. So he had a direct line to the 61 precinct. Small world. I'm sure it should have been a little more than don't worry about it kid, that's what they said to me, when it happened to me. But!!!

When I was at roll call, I'd get my assignment, I didn't talk to anyone, I'd just sit or stand in back of the Muster room. I like to get a better feel about the guys in the precinct, I would finish roll call and go to my post. I guess besides having my eyes opened and very unsure, I guess.

There was this inside police officer. One day he said hello to me that was a big relief at that time, because I knew I needed a friend. We started, I guess a friendship and more, little by little I was getting the drift, about staying away from the late tour guys. I'm still new to the precinct.

I was standing on Eastern Parkway and Rochester, my first foot assignment, when an R.M.P. pulls up. The recorder rolls down his window, looks at me and says, Cimino I like you, and so I think I'm going to back you up. MMMM, now they're playing the favorites, he also says silver is a good investment. A little while later another R.M.P. pulls up, they tell me to have a seat in the back of the car, not much talking, I got out, and I had a good feeling about this team. Later on down the road, I knew I was right; they called one guy the Colonel. He became a sergeant later on, and I met him again in my old neighborhood, Bensonhurst. Again, not much to talk about.

Since I was the new guy I had a lot of foot posts, Rochester Avenue and Eastern Parkway, Ralph and Eastern Parkway. One day tour, I'm walking Eastern Parkway, when I spot this gang of guys going into a building. So I follow them in. I'm going up the stairs, I stopped, and looked behind me, there's this guy at the bottom of the stairs. So I turn around and we both walk out, he says, let me tell you something, you never follow a gang of guys into a building alone. I didn't know what to say. I asked him his name. He said it was Mr. Brown. He says he lives on the block, he said when he saw me going into the building he followed me, he wanted to make sure I was ok. My first street teacher and one of the people watching out for the young cop, or cop. Thanks, I don't forget.

I remember one of my day tour roll calls, when it was over, I met another inside guy, he said he was in because he got shot, and maybe he talked to me because of the expression on my face. He said Al it's not going to change, just the faces change. Internally I thanked him, I think with gratitude.

I was in a car, violent dispute came over the air, another sector got there first, and it was my job. The other sector took some guy out of an apartment; he was an elderly guy, drunk. One of the cops looks at me, (he's the one that, him and his partner, had the steady foot post on Washington avenue they were supposedly taking care of the drug problem).he takes the guys wrist and brakes it with his night stick, he says here it's your collar. I take the guy to the hospital. On the way to Central Booking, I was the recorder. The guy that was locked up probably saw the expression on my face, disbelief and I felt bad for this guy. It didn't warrant that, well, he says in a clear voice, I know you didn't do it. I still didn't feel good.

Same team that backed us up on that dispute went into a store, where they sold drugs. They totaled the place. They called for a back-up we went. The one that broke this guy's wrist throws me a brown paper bag, inside the bag was a shit load of marijuana, and then they left. I told my partner how we are going to voucher this. I was riding with one of the Buddy Boys. So we went down a deserted block and threw it behind a dumpster. After the tour, I went back to the block to check if it was still there, it was gone. These guys might have been testing me to see if I was a rat. Everything was happening so fast and right in front of me, took time to compute all of this shit. Little by little I'm getting to know all the players.

Same guy told me another time. You know you have to watch out, going through a door, "you might get hit in the face with a two by four". My first threat at this precinct, not my last, this'll keep me on my toes. I didn't say anything, I just thanked him. You keep your friends close and your enemies even closer.

My old partner the one from buddy boys, we were backing them up on a toss, of a few druggies and drug dealers. He said, Al watch his hands, same team from the back-up and the bag of drugs. These two guys had the steady post on Washington Avenue. So he takes the money out of their pockets and puts it into his, then, lets them go. Nice switch. At that time my partner was still a good cop. One of these guys worn a gold shield, this meant he was a, or used to be a field training officer. Probably like Robin Hood, took from the poor and gave to them, I mean, is that how the story went, well, something like that.

I guess they wanted me to get acquainted with how the precinct works. I backed up on a dispute. When I got there, to this building, I don't remember who I was working with. When I got to the floor, I saw this guy handcuffed to the railing of a banister, he's sitting on the stairs, facing me. When from out of nowhere this cop, in what looked like army books, kicked and I mean kicked this guy in the face. I mean, again took me by surprise, out of nowhere, this cop turns and looks at me, like, what the fuck are you going to do. I'm new to this shit and haven't seen it before. This guy thought he was King, I mean the cop. Still shaking my head. What the fuck.

77 PRECINCT

F our by twelve. I was on a foot post on Rochester Avenue and Eastern Parkway. I was standing in one of the store fronts, when I spotted a department car parked. Some guy in uniform was sitting at the wheel; his back was facing me so I was standing behind the car. He gets out, comes up to me and asks what I am doing here. I think I said either standing or watching. Again he asked the same question. I probably gave him the same answer. So he leaves. I had no idea what the fuck he was talking about, or who he was. A short time later, I get a 10-2 forthwith, which means come into the house or precinct fast, so I walked back to the precinct. I stand in front of the desk; it was a lieutenant who I was familiar with. He said what did you say to Chief Brown; first, I had no idea who the guy was. I told him, he asked me what

I was doing here I told the lieutenant what I said, he said, I don't remember if the lieutenant used my first name, he said you were supposed to say, you're there to protect and something else, to that effect. He shook his head, smiled, and said get back on post. So that's what I was doing. MMMM.

I was still on foot posts. The Deputy Inspector called me into his office. This D.I. might have been the first or second D.I. to come to that precinct, and many more to follow. He said, I'm having complaints from the tenants on Rochester Avenue, between Saint John's Place and Eastern Parkway, about the crime in that area. There were burglaries, robberies, and the prostitutes. There was also this street gang in that area. Can you take that post for me, see what you can do, he said "I'll give Carte Blanche, and whatever you say goes, and whatever you need you got it." He also said it's a two man post." I guess after working with some of the do nothings, I told him I'll take the post myself. If I had to do it over again I would have enjoyed company. So I started a steady foot post.

When I was on that foot post a woman was looking out her window and called me over, she said there was this homeless guy living in the abandon building next door to her building, she was afraid that he would start a fire to keep warm, and burn down that building and her building. I said I would check it out.

I met the homeless guy one day, coming out of the building, I spoke to him; his name was Bill. Or that's what he called himself. He was a young guy in his late twenties or early thirties. I told him he couldn't stay in there. We talked, his conversation didn't make sense; he was a little out of touch with reality, but who in this neighborhood isn't. So I let him stay for some reason or another. We talked, as the days went by. I told him, you're a young man, why don't you try and get help from an organization. Then I told him, he should get into a business; I don't know how that conversation came about. After a while I didn't see him anymore.

When I stopped doing that post, I remember I was in an R.M.P., I was the recorder. Driving around, I saw him or Bill, on the corner, he was selling clothes. I told my partner to stop, I got out of the car to say hello, and to see where he got the clothes from.

He told me he got them out of the collection bin, then he went to the clothing store's garbage container, remove their wrapping, and cardboard from the clothes that they bought and they threw away the wrappings and he would wrap the clothes from the bin and was selling them on the street, not bad for a homeless guy, took my advice and opened up a business, our next entrepreneur. I guess he needed direction.

Over the course of years I use to see this youngster, he was in elementary school, nice kid. He'd stop and talk to me about school and what he was doing. Sweet kid. Every once in awhile he would tell me, how he'd get picked on and he was afraid. His name was Frankie. He would tell me, he told his mom about me and he wanted me to come over his house and meet her. On a day tour, I went over, she invited me in, we talked about her son, and how he was getting picked on, and I listened. It was nice meeting you. I think we had coffee.

When he started high school, he asked me to come up to school with him, he had no father. I guess to show that someone was looking after him, no problem; I could tell he was scared. Because the high school, Boys and Girls High was a tough school, one of the toughest in the city, even the teachers were afraid. After a while the 77 precinct asked me if I wanted to be the Truant cop in the office at the school, giving youth summons and if there was a problem. I turned it down; I didn't like being cooped up in school all day. I guess I had flash backs when I when to school, hated it.

A year or so later. I see this group of toughs walking down Eastern Parkway one carrying a garrison belt. I stopped them, he got bigger and looked tougher, it was Frankie with the belt, he looked at me, he remembered, I said stay out of trouble . . . one more kid taken by the street, either you eat or be eaten. I'll remember him as a nice kid.

Another young boy. His family lived on the block right off the precinct. He was maybe five years old at the time, his family use to sit on their stoop. He'd see me, big smile say hello, I talked to him and say hello to the family, they would just look, say nothing. In that area you almost never talked to a cop. Either because of the bad guys around, thinking that you were giving information, or they didn't trust a cop. Because they probably knew what the precinct was better than I did, at the time. You knew they were watching out for him. He would have a better chance with a family like that. He told me it was his birthday, I gave him a buck, when he did something good at school, and I'd give him a dollar too. Nice kid, nice family.

There was this cop that worked in the Seven Seven, I just got to the 77 precinct, I saw him once in the locker room changing. He was off duty, after work on a four by twelve. He stopped in a liquor store on Atlantic Ave. He buys what he has to. Comes out, gets robbed and shot. They say he was ambushed. Whoever did it, took his gun and shield. That was the first police officer's funeral I went to. Putting this in, they said he was a nice quiet guy. Hey I remembered.

Now it was test time for the new kid on the block, talking about my foot post of Rochester Ave. There was this street gang Ally-Baba and the Forty Thieves. They were into robberies and burglaries. I'm not saying that these were the guys but a few in the pack could have been, they started hanging out on Eastern Parkway off Rochester. I told them to move, they would move and come back, next day told them to move again, they move and come back, third day same thing. This time, one of them had a wise mouth, so I hit him once knocked him on his ass, this time they left. The kid I hit comes back with his father and the crew. The father starts yelling, you hit my son, the whole nine yards. I start yelling if he keeps hanging out with these guys he's going to get locked up, the father stopped, look at me, took the kid home. They never showed up on my post again, except for this one big kid, he would just pass by and smile, with this kid.

There was a robbery that went down, I thought it might have been him, so when I saw him, I told him to meet me in the precinct the next day at one o'clock. I'm sure it was my day off, I even told him what it was for,.sure as shit, he was there the next day, at one in the afternoon. We cleared it up, it wasn't him, he knew it wasn't him, I could tell he like the recognition and he could tell the boys

50

what had happened. Hey putting a smile on someone face, that's what it's about. I think

Another time I had a tenant from one of the buildings; he let me stay in his apartment and look through the window and check the street from the inside of his house. He said if they ever found out what he was doing, that he would be killed, he still let me do it, an old timer.

There were prostitutes in one of the buildings on Eastern Parkway. A girl walked out of one of the buildings, she crossed Eastern Parkway and into the 71 precinct and did her thing on the street, stopping cars trying to turn a trick. I'm on the opposite corner. She's looking at me, smiling, she was probably saying, he can't do nothing, I'm not in his precinct, they probably knew the boundary of the precinct better than most. I said to myself, what the fuck am I this stupid, so I 10—85 a car, meaning I needed a car for assistance when they arrived I got in the back. I tell them go around Lincoln Terrace park, that's where she was hooking. The Colonel and his partner respond. We come up alongside of her. I get out of the car, said you're under arrest. She tells me you can't do this, it's not your precinct. Again the shield trick, see City of New York, we took her in.

I tell the desk sergeant, I going to give her a discon-summons for impeding auto traffic, he tells me to give her a D.A.T., [desk appearance ticket,] I tell him I'm giving her a discon-summons. Now he orders me to arrest her. Now I wanted to see if my Carte Blanche is going to work. I see the D.I., I told him what's going on, he goes to the desk sergeant, he tells him, he does whatever he wants. Discon summons given. That also ended my chance for getting into Anti Crime, he was the Anti Crime sergeant. The Inspector, man of his word. Smiling.

When I was doing this post I use to walk out of my area and walk along Eastern Parkway to Utica Ave, more people around. On Eastern Parkway, there was a McDonalds' there on Eastern and Utica Avenue, right next to the McDonalds there was a Muslims building or it might have been another Mosque. I went up the stairs, knocked on the door, a guy came out. He was wearing a turbid and what looked like a smock. I ask him what are you guys are about; he looks at me, goes back in, comes back out and gives me a book. Then he goes back in. I started to read it. It told me all of what they were about. I walked to that area a few times.

One time I went into the McDonalds, there was this guy there doing security, I noticed him a few times going into the Mosque next to the McDonalds, he was pushing around some guy. I asked what's wrong. He said this guy sells drugs here and we don't like it. I told him I would take care of it. This guy he was pushing around looked like a bum. I took him outside, the guard followed. I gave this guy a shove and on his ass he went, I told him don't come back. I told the security guard, that's my job, and left. These Mosques people don't want trouble or to bring attention to themselves. So they take care of their own business, I guess, there way, because they don't want to be involved with the police.

Again a bit of information. There was this guy I met on my post would tell me things, ride his bike, laugh and walk away. He was a little annoying, so I took his name; he's telling me that he was an informant for the detectives. I went to see the detectives, told them about him, and he was. I'm not sure, but once, he steered me to a guy who had information, this guy was one of the local drunks, he was sitting on the ground against a building, pretending to be annoyed, but was talking, of things going down. Again these people that talk to the police, can and will be killed by the toughs on the street. Or anyone is doing bad things. But they took a chance because they didn't like dirt either.

I did that for several months and I wanted off, I was getting bored. So I started to ride in cars with a different guy almost every day, one worse than the other. Guys who didn't want to work and guys who didn't want to pick up jobs, these guy really didn't give a fuck. Some of the bosses didn't give a shit either. You had cops and bosses, as soon as they came into the precinct, as fast as they came in, they would put 57s in, to get out. A fifty seven is paper work to be transferred out of the precinct, to another house. That's how bad it was.

I started to get disillusioned. After riding with empty suits, [empty suits guys who wore a uniform and did nothing], I guess it showed, I thought this was the job, I couldn't figure it out, I'm slow as they come, until one day, a radio team came over. I used to see these guys around, we didn't talk that much a little nod, a smile, they said Al, these guys your riding with, are the left over's, they don't want to do anything, you got to get yourself a partner. I mean, me, slow on the up take. That team was one of the best in the precinct. Down the road they watched out for me, Italian guys. They made my first Christmas dinner at the precinct.

There was this one guy who just got out of Anti Crime; he was looking for a partner so we hook-up. He was going to show me the ropes. So we're doing a four by twelve, we meet this other sector in this parking lot. All of a sudden, the wine comes out the joints come out, I said to myself, "self, what the fuck", so I drink a little wine and had a few hits. Don't get me wrong I smoked pot before on was on the job, but the way I felt, I knew this was wrong. I thought if I ever had to use my weapon, I wanted to make sure; it was me, not the pot or the drinking that did the shooting. That was the first and that was the last for both of us. As matter of fact these two guys that had the pot and wine, from, a well known source, were taking money from drug dealers, they put on a good front of doing good. This was the same team who broke the guy's wrist. This guy, the guy I teamed up with, the only thing he had on his mind was women. He was dating to girls at once, and every day it was the same conversation. One had money and average looks the other had looks but no money. If he had to choose he didn't know who he'd marry, what would I do? Told him I was married and I didn't know. Today wonder who he chose?

I remember we were riding down Franklin Avenue, a very hot summer day, and windows down no air conditioning in the car. We're moving slowly, I was the recorder. I turn my head for a second and looked out the window, just in time, as this female, was running and she was about to dive in my window of the R.M.P., she had two knives in her hands, points of the knives pointed at me, as she takes the dive, I pushed open the door, slam it into her stomach or chest. I could hear my partner yelling "shoot her, shoot her" as he jumps out of the car, I jumped out and disarmed her. He's asking me, "Why didn't you shoot her?" Why didn't you shoot her?" I did the first thing I thought of, I don't know, next stop Kings County Hospital G-building. The G-building at Kings County Hospital is the building all the pick-up E.D.P.'s [emotionally disturbed persons] is driven to before they are admitted or sent home. Better there than dead. Decisions Decisions Decisions.

Just before I hooked-up with my partner I mentioned I lived just one block outside the 77 precinct, I had a Sheppard dog. When I'd come home from a four by twelve, I'd walk the dog. There used to be this one prostitute on the corner, she use to tell me," I saw your wife, she walked the dog and she went back in the house", everything alright." nice looking out. Hey we all have to make a living right or wrong some just can't help it.

Another time I'm outside sitting on the stoop, this guy from next door, I knew he didn't live there, he was sweeping the side walk, I mean, and he looked paranoid. He's looking at me and looking all around as if he's being watched. He starts talking out loud as if not talking to me, he says, you're a cop, I have information about two murders, and I know the guy who did it, he hands me a piece of paper and tells me to meet him there tomorrow night at that address at 9pm, then goes inside.

I figured either he could be some nut job or good information. I say to myself let me get some advice. Next day I talked to one of the detectives, he was a sergeant; we were talking outside in the parking lot of the 77 precinct. I tell him what I have, he said if I were you I wouldn't do anything, I told him I didn't feel right not doing anything, I left.

I still didn't know who to trust, I had two guys on my mind, but I let it go. They were a black team who was in R.I.P. [Robbery Enforcement Program]. So the next night comes, I mean, till this day I feel bad, what I put my wife through, she's totally not in my game, totally out of her league. I tell her what I have, tell her where I'm going, then I tell her if I'm not back within a reasonable amount of time, to let the guys know, which is the police department, where to start looking for me.

The thing that came to my mind about me going there alone was, I remembered reading this story years ago in the papers, there was this detective on a case, if I remember the story correct, the department didn't know why he was down there, In the Village in Manhattan. Whether he was investigating something on his own or something else. I guess maybe that's why that story popped in my head, anyway. They found him chopped up down in the village, and was put in plastic bags. Nice, that's what I thought was going too happened to me if it was a set-up, nice I need this.

All of a sudden my mind starts working. I go to this apartment in the 79 precinct, I think second or third floor, I look for the apartment number, I knock on the door he opens up, he's nervous as ever, There's all types of radio equipment and tuners, in this room that I'm in, a couch, and a four foot mirror leaning against a wall opposite me, I sit on the couch, sitting forward, I have my weapon in my ankle holster, that's where my hand was near, he's looking at me, there's a door across from me, he goes in and shuts the door. I'm leaning forward, unsnapped my ankle holster and have my hand on my gun, I tell you it was a long moment, he comes out, and he seemed a little more relaxed. He tells me this was on his mind for a long time and he can't keep it to himself any longer, so he gives me the name of the guy who killed these other two guys, gives me the around about date, gives me the address where they were killed, and the names of the two guys that were killed. It was like a big weight was taken off his shoulders. I found out later he was a relative of the people living next door from me, so they had to tell him I was a police officer.

Everything was done on my own time. When I found out that the address where the double homicide took place, It was somewhere in the 69 precinct. I went to the precinct, I identify myself, and I wanted to talk to the detectives or the detective who was involved in this case. I went upstairs to the squad, I'm asking questions, when this detective from out of nowhere, gets in my face and starts muscling me. An old time detective comes between us, and he hands me this homicide book, this book is where they keep a listing of the solved and unsolved homicide cases in the precinct . . . I started looking through the book, I find the homicide case I was looking for. It states, cased solved or closed. So I show it to the old timer, he looks, he gives me the detectives name and phone number that handled the case, I called him, I tell him about this informant I had. I told him the story that was told to me. He says the case is closed, he said he put the crime on a person who was killed by a car. He sounded a little off beat, and he didn't want to know any more and I left. I'll be running into the detective who got in my face in the future. Another murder solved, or lets play spin the bottle. Ah!

Another time I came home from a four to twelve, my wife was sleeping. I laid down for a little while; I was still wound up from the tour. So I sat up and relax, when I heard this commotion outside. I see these two 88 precinct cops chasing this guy. I was wearing a sweat suit and slippers. I see this guy go into a building the two cops follow. So I went downstairs, I'm standing on my stoop. I see the guy climb out the front window of the building he just ran into, as he comes out the window, I start moving down the steps, he runs across the street onto the sidewalk and I jumped him, we both go over a fence, thank god, me on top of him. I'm about to nail him, but the expression on his face, told me he had it.

The two 88 precinct cops come running over. I don't remember if I told them that I was on the job. I got up, and they cuffed him. I left and went back upstairs. My wife woke, said hello, I laid in bed. I'll tell you we were the only three white people on the block. There were a few people on the block that I started to get to know, Shorty, well known drinker, Lenny well known drinker and possibly drug user or past user.

At first, they were suspicious of me, because of me being a cop, then they started to look out for me, I mean small things, like after a twelve by eight tour. I would come home tired, park the car on the wrong side of the street, I would forget about alternate side of the street parking. They would ring the bell, one, or the other, wake me to move my car, little bullshit like that, Lenny died a little later on. Me personally nice people on the block the ones I knew.

My wife at the time came home from work one day. I'm telling you these incidents, in relation to Brooklyn North cops, compared to Brooklyn South police officers, I saw her face. I asked her what's wrong, she says nothing. I tell her," I can see it, there's something wrong, what's wrong, "she's a nervous wreck, she worked around the Court street area, she tells me, this truck with four guys in it, the driver backed up and he hit her car. They get out; threaten to punch her in the face. I tell her, "Get your coat on", we got in her car. We went to the area where it happened, she points out the truck. I told her to stay here; she was about three quarters of a block away from where the truck was. I walked over, to the truck. It was a fish truck, making a delivery to a Chinese restaurant. I tell them," who's the guy that threatened to punch my wife in the face because of an accident". These four black guys they jumping up and down and yelling at me. OK, I leave.

I walk into the restaurant, I tell them I'm a cop, and I used their phone, I dialed 911. I tell the operator, I'm an off duty police officer. Can I have a 10—85; off duty needs a back-up. I tell the operator, tell them no light and sirens, come in slow, I go outside, I see two R.M.P. easing around the corner. They stopped. I tell them what went down; they asked them where's the guy that threatened his wife. They pointed, he's upstairs in the building. Three police officers stayed down, one comes up with me. There's a guy up there, this cop that's with me, turns his back and leaves the room.

I said," you're the fucking guy that threaten my wife over a fucking accident," this guy picks up a lamp and was going to hit me with it, so I took out my gun, he says," you're not going to shoot me," he puts down the lamp. I put away my gun, and punch him in the face. I split my knuckle open. The cop that came up with me, comes back in, he says, is everything OK? I said," yea" we both go downstairs. The other cops look at me, they says, we can't find the driver of the truck, do you want us to voucher the truck and all this stuff," I say "no, thanks guys, "they leave, I go back to my wife.

No problem, it was only a small dent, condition corrected. Ah, love this country.

Where I worked and lived in. This area of the precinct was a very high crime area, and I mention it. The reason I lived there, was because, my ex wife's uncle had a house in that area for years, he offered us an apartment for fifty dollars a month after we get married, we took him up on his offer

One day I was leaving to do a four by twelve, had my dry cleaning in one hand, I was opening the front door of the hallway. I see this guy cuffed to my stairway railing, a guy standing next to him. I said what's up. I'm a cop from the 77 precinct, he says can you watch this guy, I can't find my partner, this cop was in plain clothes, no problem. Now he leaves, now I'm with the perp. I'm standing there, when an R.M.P. pulls up from the precinct, I tell them," I'm on the job, and ready to go to work in the 77." I tell them that a plain clothes officer has this collar, he couldn't find his partner and he went to look for him; he asked me if I could watch this guy. So I tell them, if they can watch him, I have to get to work, again no problem. Never know when something is going to happen. More likely in a place like this then another area. I got to work on time. Again chain reaction, A to B to C then to work.

I get a foot post around Saint. Johns and Utica avenue, doing a day tour. I'm hanging out near this pizza place, the owners are telling me, yea I'm Italian your Italian, yea, yea yea yea, we gotta stick together. I go outside, there's this kid about eighteen years old. He pulls up his jacket sleeves; he has a whole load of watches on his arm. I ask him does he have receipts for those watches, well we get in a little tussle, I end up falling in the street, I slipped on some grease, he lands on top of me and we're rolling around, he gets up and takes off, I start chasing him down St. Johns, I call for an 85 forthwith, this detective in uniform picks me up, we start looking for him. We can't find him. We go back to the precinct; I make out a U.F. 61 complaint report.

I tell you my emotions flooded between embarrassment my pride, fear and all that other good stuff, you'd figure I'm on the ground, where were my Pisano's from the pizza place. From that day on they couldn't even look at me, I'm talking about the pizza guys. Then I thought, if they did help, there goes their business. It took me quite awhile to get back into the swing of things, and get my composure back. I didn't know what to feel until it settled, I think a little fear and embarrassment took over until I overcame it.

Well anyway. I would say about a good month passed with this incident. I'm parked with my partner, the one who was in Anti Crime, right near the pizza place, when who shows up out of nowhere, it's this black team I was telling you about, from R.I.P., they say Al, this is the guy that assaulted you and here's his address. I was flooded with emotions again; I don't know maybe I forgot about closure. Hey I human.

So me and my partner go to this address, he's not there. We talk to his sister. I tell her what he's wanted for, I tell her, to tell him, to meet me at the precinct tomorrow.

He comes in, I'm there, I sat him down in the muster room, I said," you remember me", he's says yea and nods, I said you know what I can do to you right now, he nods, I look at him. I gave him a break. I thought about the grease, and I needed a new pair of shoes. I told him to go home. R.I.P., (robbery enforcement program) thanks guys

Me and my partner worked together for about eight months, before we split, and I think he went back into Anti Crime. I remembered when I was a kid twice police officers gave me a break, maybe this time it was mine turn to give. I hope it helped, I know it helped me.

My first Christmas at this precinct, we have a new Deputy Inspector. These two cops, the ones that told me, I should get a partner, both, Italian guys. They told me that they came to back me up one tour because they heard my voice change, when I was talking on the radio; they figured I might need a backup. Nice looking out, nice paying attention. So they decided to cook macaroni and clams, fresh clams, and if I want in, I said "yes," they did all the cooking, we ate in shifts. When it was your turn to eat, the other sectors would cover your sector. So it was my turn and we're eating, there's a gallon of wine, it's on the floor. Who walks in, the Deputy Inspector, who could be a hard nose, so they invited him to eat, he says yes, we're looking at each other, you know about the wine, so I invited him to have a class of wine, I guess someone had to do it, we're all waiting, he said yes, sigh of relief, he ate, we ate and had a glass of wine. He said thank you, left, said nothing. Next team, good dinner guys.

He's the same D.I. that called me into his office and said that" he admired my fortitude", I thank him, I didn't quite get the true meaning of it then, but as I look back now, I remember what you said, and now it gives me comfort knowing someone took an interest, and gave me some recognition. Thanks again.

I worked with this one cop, who just transferred here, quiet guy, mild mannered. Day tour. We picked up what seemed to be a fight in the street, we called it in. We stop, get out of the car. One guy is tussling with this other guy on the ground, he said it was his friend; he was having some kind of a fit. So we were trying to hold him down, he's kicking, the cop I'm with is standing in front of this guy with his hands in his pockets, standing in front of his legs, for some reason as I'm trying to control the guy on the ground, I stood, twisted around, there's this guy, right at my back, with a knife in his hand pointed at my back, if I didn't turn around he would have stabbed me in the back, it didn't register what was happening, I disarmed him, like a fucking idiot, I went back to the guy on the ground.

I saw a sergeant and his driver, they were watching the whole thing, and they were standing in the street, about 25 feet away, just looking. I'm sure they saw the guy with the knife. I knew this sergeant and driver didn't like me, from the start. Fuck you, after the guy settled, I went back to the precinct, told the deck officer, I can't ride with this guy, he's going to get me killed.

A short time later this cop was transferred to 84 precincts, into Central Booking, that's the precinct where they do all the arrest bookings. I met him there some time later; I thought he was going to be pissed, he was happy as pig in shit to be there. That's the last time I saw him. Nooo! They wouldn't stab a cop in the back.

Sometime later at the Whitestone Pound, the lieutenant told me you know, there are cops, who would let something happen, just to be hero's, than I thought about the sergeant and his driver, maybe they wanted to be hero's. For that day, shooting a perp that stabbed a cop. Food for thought.

At around the time when the precinct was christened the Alamo, there was this article in Newsday, stated that the 77 precinct had more killings that year, than that of the state of Rhode Island; I think for that year we had 87 homicides. A little bit of trivial information.

I was at Kings County Hospital "G building". I brought in an E D P, [emotional disturbed person] I had to wait there until they processed her; it was a twelve by eight. All the E.D.P.'s were behind a brick wall, maybe the wall was about four foot high. I was in a chair leaning back up against a four foot partition where the clerical staff was, I was facing the E.D.P.'s. I'm leaning back my eyes were half closed; my chair was near the opening where a person could walk through and talk to the clerical people. I see this guy walking down the hallway, I spotted him out of the corner of my eye, his jacket moves open and I see, what looked like a kitchen knife in his pants, handle sticking out, he walks passed me.

As soon as the steps through the opening and faces the receptionist desk, I take him down from the rear, we're fighting on the floor, I'm trying to take the knife away, now I'm on top of this guy fighting and there's a hospital police officer standing above us, saying now what's your name, and I'm saying to myself same time, same place, different worlds' I finally disarmed him; I gave the collar to another hospital police officer, who had more medals than God. After I get up brush myself off the receptionist looks at me, she says nothing. But by the look on her face she knew he could have pulled the knife out and put it in her chest. I gave myself a pat on the back.

Another time I was there I was sitting with the E.D.P.'s I'm taking to one of the woman there. I was inside the fence, she has what looks like a scarf or a sweater on the lap, she moves and a knife falls to the floor, like who did this search. I gave it to the hospital guards. Never know, unless you do it yourself.

Day tour. I had a foot post on Eastern Parkway. Someone comes up to me and tells me, something is happening at the bank on Eastern and Utica avenue, I try to put it over the air, my radio is not working. As I'm getting closer to the bank, I give this guy a dime, I tell him to call 911, tell them a police officer needs assistance at the bank, hey, you gota trust someone, I get inside the bank, everyone standing, facing this one guy, he's carrying a case or backpack, I spot him, he looks at me. I get the sense, he doesn't like authority, so I take my hat off and start walking towards him and talking to him. As I'm walking and talking I'm moving him towards a corner of the banks where there's no people. I was trying to isolate him. When I get him there, the boys from two different precincts storm in. One guy who used to work at my precinct, starts taking over, as if I wasn't even there, I said hey, I'm here, I got his attention, he came down to earth, like I wanted to say, who the fuck are you, but, you know, now we'll talk, I tell him what we have, I gave him the collar. He wasn't from the 77 precinct.

Another day tour. Riding with a young cop, got a job, man with gun, in front of a building. When we get there we pull the R.M.P. directly across from a guy, he was looking at a crowd across from him. He had a nice size bag strapped over his left shoulder with his right hand inside the bag. My partner takes cover behind the R.M.P.; I do a crouch position in the street, gun out. I heard this one voice in the crowd yelling," shoot him, he has a gun shoot him." I felt like the person who was yelling, shoot him, wanted us to shoot him, for other reasons. The guy takes his hand out of the bag; he had no gun in his hand. I go across check him out, he had no gun. I turned to the crowd I see the guy who was yelling. I started walking towards him, he took off. The only thing I could think of, he might have had a thing for this guy, made the call and wanted us to do his dirty work, gut feeling, or it might have been nothing more than a big mouth.

It was a day tour I handled a job, see complainant in one of the projects. We go the apartment they gave us. We talked to the complainant she says her daughter, went into the elevator, when two boys, stopped the elevator, knocked her to the floor and raped her. She gives us there names and description, I don't remember if it was that day, or the day before that the rape happened, because I don't remember taking her to the hospital for a checkup or taking her clothes. The girl was slow. I called for a back up. We went to the apartment; we talked to the mother of the person we were going to arrest. The other team goes to another apartment. We take a boy and his mother to the precinct. She's told what occurred. This is a rape first degree. The riding D.A. is called down to the 77 precinct this kid was as hard as nails. The riding D.A. does all the questioning, basically my job was done. For this arrest, we put in for a medal, paper work and all. I don't know, maybe a week later, the D.I. talks to me, he says, that he can only give me and my partner the medals, not the other team, I told him that's ok, if the other team couldn't get it, I didn't need the medal. Thanks anyway.

It was a day tour; I went on a detail . . . The location was in Harlem. I remember they gave me this avenue. There was a divider in the middle where you can sit on, like a curb or stay until the traffic was gone. This one Captain tells me, I want no one sitting on the divider, OK. So I'm walking around on this one block location, making sure it stayed clean from people sitting. So I'm at one end of the block, when I get back there's this homeless guy sitting on my curb. I say, ok you've got to move, he looks up, and does nothing, so I get myself into position and tell him again, as I'm telling him a radio car pulls up to the opposite side of the curb, the driver waves to me to come over. I'm walking over to the R.M.P., there's a different captain in the car, he says what's wrong, and I tell him. Now he says, ok, just leave him. I tell him, another captain just told me, he wants no one sitting on the middle divider, I told him, you two guys got to get your acts together. He looks at the driver like, what, let's go, they drove off. When I went back the person, he was gone and so were the captain and the R.M.P.

I was doing a day tour with a young police officer, who later on went into plain clothes. We made a collar, did the paperwork, and we're on our way to Central Booking, I was driving. We're going down Flatbush Avenue, to Central Booking, when to the left, I see on one of the blocks, a commotion. I make a left turn and stop the car and we end up making a robbery collar, no weapon. We take down the complainant info. I don't remember if we gave the complainant a lift to Central Booking or we told him to meet us there. Well anyway when we got there, the complainant was there and my partner took the collar. Pays to drive with tunnel vision, or have a meter for car service.

There was a big thing in the area with chain snatches. This is how much balls these guys had. Warm day on Atlantic avenue, cars, traffic, people's windows down, slow moving, driver relaxing, kid spots a chain around her neck. Walks up to the car and grabs the chain from around her neck, she in shock. When you don't know you don't know. Same thing windows down, handbag on passenger side seat, guy passing by looking in cars, you don't think of these things, hand comes in, bag goes out.

I was riding with another guy, four by twelve. Before we went out, they said a Senator was coming to the precinct, a very well known Senator. He was going to be driven around by an inside detective and a female police officer, both were black cops, she was a female Reverend. I spoke to her a few times, Godly person, very nice too, the male detective, nice, friendly. He told me once, at the time when all the killings of the cab drivers in Manhattan was happening, he drove a cab as a decoy. He was the second cop that told me this. The first police officer that told me this was a cop, or he made detective from the 60 precinct. That night myself and my partner get a gun run, two guys on this corner, one having a gun, we get the job, we get there first. We're patting these two guys down. The detective rides up; they were the back-up team. Just by the way he was acting, the female was following him, and they were both out of the car, creeping up slowly. We had both of these guys up against the car. When they saw us, they got back into the car, pulled next to us. I looked at the Senator, the Senator looks back at me, I see a look on his face like, then I hear the Senator say," take me back to the precinct."

When I saw this male detective back at the precinct. I told him, as I was passing," you know you were show boating" he said nothing and kept walking. He's the same guy that was first on the scene when I called a 10-85 near the pizza place, he was driving an R.M.P., I jumped in and we did a search.

I was doing a day tour, driving down Atlantic Avenue, going from Vanderbilt Avenue to Ralph Avenue. I was passing all the collision shops along the way. In front of this one shop, there was this Cadillac Eldorado parked in front of the shop, on the sidewalk. for you to pass the shop, if you were walking, you had to walk in the street. This wasn't the first time I saw that car parked on the sidewalk. I'm driving, so I stopped the R.M.P., one of the guys, I'm sure he was the owner. I told him," to move the car". He says," I take care of all the cops, so it stays there", and gives me a smirk. I said," you don't take care of me", I have my window rolled down and he's leaning against the door of my car. I tried to get out of the car and he pushes the door closed, I pushed the door back open, get out, throw him up against the car and put the cuffs on him, you're under arrest.

I take him back to the precinct. We're in the Muster room, we were sitting at the table and I'm writing out a summons. Some cops were telling me this guy does favors for some of the cops, I said nothing. One of the Anti-Crime sergeants comes in, and tells me to give him a break," No Serge, this guy pushed me". The sergeant walked away. Whatever they did after that was not my problem. Possible they might have taken the summons out of the summons box and threw it away. Possible, wouldn't be the first time. There goes my career in Anti-Crime . . . again, this time different Sergeant.

Sometime after. Another day tour. The D.I., the one they say came out of retirement to take over the 77 precinct. He came into the roll call room and tells me he wants twenty five parkers on Atlantic Avenue, I said ok. I go out and in between jobs I'm writing summons on Atlantic Avenue. You know blocked driveway, parked on sidewalk, double parkers, etc. I get to this one collision place, there's this car that was parked perpendicular to the building, blocking the whole sidewalk. I get out I'm about to give it a summons, when this police officer comes out. I knew him from the 77 precinct, he works there. We didn't talk much, he said," that's my car". I tell him, I think they called him fish, I guess because he was a swimmer," I'm banging all the collisions places and cars on Atlantic Avenue, now this is going to make me look like shit." I said, "You have to move it". I mean he's pissed, rather than look at it my way. I said [name] "I'll be back in five minutes, if it's still here you're getting a summons", we drive away. I looked at my watch, I came back in five, and the car was gone.

When I went back to the precinct, me and this cop that owned the car, that I said I was going to a summons to, we're passing in the back of the precinct foyer, going in opposite directions. He looked at me, I got the feeling that he wanted to jump on me, and then I think he thought twice about it. No common sense. That day I told the D.I. that I could have only given out eight parkers, it was too busy. He said, "Did you take yourself off the air"? I told him, "I didn't think about taking myself off the air." He walked away. You know word got around.

Same thing happened at the other end of the precinct, around Washington Avenue. Again car parked on the sidewalk. I told the person in charge to move it. He starts laughing at me." I'm not moving it; it's the sergeant's car". I told him, "I'll be back in five minutes", the five minute trick, gives them time to think, if it not moved it's getting a summons. I came back in five minutes, the car was moved. We're driving around; we get a 10-02 forthwith, back to the house. We pull into the parking lot, whose there, the sergeant, I know he's pissed. I get out of the car, walked up to him, he says," that was my car", I say Serge, "This guy starts laughing at me" and says he's not moving the car", what would you have done? He put his head down and walked away. That was it. I liked this guy too. Later he became a Lieutenant.

Day tour driving down Eastern Parkway, From Ralph to Vanderbilt direction. When I see this tow truck parked on the sidewalk on the center aisle of the parkway, just parked, the driver standing next to the truck. I stopped the car, and asked him what he was doing, he said nothing. I told him to get the truck off the sidewalk, he gave me some snotty answer He's another guy that says he does work for some of the guys in the precinct. I knew most of the guys were from the Buddy Boys crowd. I asked to see his license and registration, he says no. I told him you're under arrest, he said you can't do this, and started to walk away, so I jumped on him, brought him down, and cuffed him. I don't mind if guys do work for some of the cops., But when another cop speaks or asks you a question, don't treat him like shit because you got the back-up of some of the guys at the precinct, not my fault if you're a dick.

We went to the house and I was writing a discon summons, a few of the guys wanted me to give him a break, I thought he was a smart ass, and getting a little too big, for not responding to a police officer in the right way. So he got the summons. Again whatever they did after that. I did my job. From that day on if looks could kill, from this tow driver I'd be dead. But from then on he acted correct when I was around.

Another time I'm riding with my ex partner from Buddy Boys. We were on St. Johns Place and he sees a Newsday truck taking all the lights. We stopped the driver, he gives him a load of red light summons, he asked me if I wanted any. I don't remember if I joined in. The driver said that they always did this. That's another no no. This is when we first hooked up. You live and learn.

Another day tour. I had a sector. I went up to the front desk, and told the desk officer I wasn't in the mood for a sector, could he give me an easy post around Plaza Street. The scenery and the buildings were a lot better to look at. So I'm walking down one of the blocks, this gang is coming up in the opposite direction. I stopped and they surrounded me. I'm in the middle of a circle, one of them comes face to face with me, I look him in the eyes, he drops his head, and they leave. I continued walking; I stopped on one of the corners on Eastern Parkway, and start talking to this guy. As I'm talking, I'm looking over his shoulder, I see the same gang arguing with another guy, his friends are standing by. I start walking over, as I approach them, they start running towards Eastern Parkway, in my direction. The guy they were arguing with is on the ground. I start running after them. I put over the air my post number, I'm chasing about ten to fifteen youths. There must have been a party at the precinct, because, it looked like the whole precinct came backing me up. They probably figured I rarely ask for a back-up, so they knew it had to be something. The guys stopped the gang about two blocks from the location. One of the guys they had was either hit with an ax or a hammer. I took both of them to the hospital. I found out later that one had about six puncture wounds to his body. I came back to do the paperwork. I told the sergeant that was on the scene. I think it was the sergeant whose car was parked on the sidewalk, what had happened, he said make it cross a complaint, and lock them both up. The courts will figure it out. Thanks guys. These were the same guys who surrounded me; they were looking for trouble and found it. The desk sergeant said, Al, thought you wanted a nice easy day. Yea, nice easy day, to smell the flowers.

When you walk into the 77 precinct from the front door lobby, you'd come through two double doors and there would be a row of metal chairs, they were all hooked together. One day a guy comes in and sits, the next day the same thing. After a while he was like a fixture, nobody paid any attention to him, figuring maybe he'll go away. Well I'm paying attention. Next time I noticed he had a couple of bags. Next time a few more bags. I go into the Deputy Inspectors office, this D.I. was the one that was at the Christmas dinner. I tell him, "You're going to have a hard time getting rid of this guy that's outside. To me, it looks like he moved in", and I walked out. The D.I. comes out, calls two cops over and tells them to ask him to leave, so they ask him to leave, he refuses, before you know it, they're dragging him into the Muster room. They cuffed him and called for a bus, probably to Kings County Hospital. Most likely the G building. [G building is where you send the E.D.P.'S] Or for people who sit in one spot to long, and make claim to that area.

Same thing with this girl. She'd sit there; she was in her late teens or early twenties, same clothes, very sweet. You could tell that she could be taken advantage of. Slow witted. I didn't see her for a while, till one day she came back to the precinct, she looked pregnant. Yea they said she was raped. Nothing new. Felt sorry for her that's all you

77 PRECINCT

'm driving a Sergeant, who was not too long in the precinct. We're going down one of the blocks, we stopped at the stop sign, there's this guy, on the opposite corner, facing us. I said serge," Something's going down", he says, in a little excited voice, how do you know. I moved the car up, throw it in park, two guys are running in our direction, we jumped out grab them. They just robbed someone. We cuffed them. We put in the back seat and went back to the precinct.

We did a fast pat down. We brought them into the precinct. About ten minutes later, he tells me to check the back seat, between the seats where they were sitting. I found a toy gun. We didn't know if it was there prior to the guys in the back, or they put it there. We made the arrest. He says," how did you know something was happening, "I told him," the guy on the corner smoking the cigarette," he was looking at us, and blowing the smoke out of the left side of his mouth". Smoking is bad for your health.

Late tour, driving with a young cop, dispute on Eastern Parkway. We get to the location. There's a woman standing next to a fence, with a man facing her. They are facing each other. He has a knife up over his head, and he's about to plunge what looked like a kitchen knife into her chest. We're out of the car. I'm lead, my partners behind me, guns drawn. The guy with the knife is in like, a frozen position. Another guy jumps in front of me carrying a baby, he's telling me," don't shoot him, don't shoot". I'm maybe six to eight feet from the situation. I put my gun away, when I see the man with the knife, I'll call it; he broke concentration, that's when

I attack him. I took him down and disarmed him. My partner's right behind me punches him in the face. My partner took the collar. Good solid wake-up call. I'm sure my partner was into the arts. Better a punch in the face, than a bullet. Again, decisions, decisions, decisions.

I'm driving with a young cop. he was a past Golden Glover. Nice soft spoken guy, we get a call meet the ambulance at the hospital. We get to the emergency room, and we see this female. I mean she looks like she was beaten with a stick, her husband did this and she refused to press charges. You knew she was afraid. Thank God they passed a law a short time ago, that if it's a felony assault on a spouse, the Police Officer's didn't need the wife's permission to arrest the husband, account of them being afraid, and the seriousness of the assault. We raced to that address, where she lived. We meet the ambulance team that took her to the hospital, going up the stairs. We didn't know that they were going there; I mean they were pissed, we told them, this is our job, and they looked and turned around. I got the feeling that they thought we weren't going to be there, or take the husband.

Let me say that there were several ambulance teams that I met in that area, some were better that the others, some got involved, these guys from my past experience were the best. As you can see . . . we go into this apartment, this guy is in front of us maybe about eight or nine feet away, and he is still pumped, the young cop was behind me, I knew he was backing me up, because the perp was looking over my shoulder, I tell him we could make this easy or we could make this hard. He took the easy way. One under, young cop took collar.

I told you about the inside police officer that I became friends with me. Artie Boor. I use to get pissed at certain shit. He said, "Your job is to arrest them, the court does the punishment, and you can't help everyone." I never forgot that. Made my life a lot easier and less aggravating. When he retired we kept in touch for a number of years after that, he went from the Police Department, right into the Post Office. One of the nicest, gentlest guys you'd ever want to meet. It was my pleasure to have known him.

I was doing a day tour 10—85, meet some police officer at a certain location, it was on Eastern Parkway. We get there we meet a team of plains clothes officers from the City and State task force, they said they had information that a guy wanted, was at this address. I asked them if they had a folder on this guy, they give me a folder and a picture. I ran a quick scan and from what I read he was a bad guy. We go to the door and I knocked, the lead says, "open it's the superintendent". Right there I know we're in trouble a building like this definitely has no super. So when they open the door, everybody goes in. I take a position where there's cover because you know if he's there and he has a gun we're in trouble, just by the super remark. Everyone goes through the apartment he's not there. We'll get him next time.

Another time I'm driving with this rookie, this is the one who wanted to be a fireman. It a four by twelve.10—85 meet warrants. We get there; spoke to the warrant police officers the bad guy is in this apartment, first floor. My partner and the warrant guys go through the front door, I go around the back of the building, to the courtyard, I found the window and apartment he was supposed to be in. They would give me enough time to get there. So I'm by myself in the rear, pitch black, except for the lights coming out of the blinds of the windows that had lights on, it was still very dark, and cold. I kneel down in a cover position, waiting, it's starting to get cold. I'm waiting and waiting. I gave them enough time. So I go back to the front of the building. There's the rookie and the warrant officers, they were talking out front. Do you think my partner comes back and gets me? Easily distracted, Al you're on your own. I was pissed, didn't say a word. Just talking to myself. Again Self.

I was working a day shift. Radio car and another different partner for the day. A radio run came over then air, I don't remember what kind of job, and I was driving. I know it was light and sirens, on Eastern Parkway. I was on the service road. I guess as you become more and more familiar with what you doing, you see a lot more. On the service road, there are cars parked on both sides of the street. So it's only one lane of traffic. I'm driving, looking ahead, I saw a little girl, I would say, maybe five or six years of age, she was standing next to another little girl maybe two or three years old, the older girl was probably watching the younger one. They're standing at the curb; I'm just seeing the little girls' heads and maybe part of her shoulders, because of the cars parked there. Now I see the older girl and don't see the younger of the two, I spotted her coming out from the end of the car and into the street. I drove the R.M.P. into a parked car on the opposite side of the street, with my right hand, I put it on my partner's chest, it's automatic with me, or I got it from the Seinfeld show. I didn't have time to tell him what I was doing, he probably saw it to.

The older one either let go of her hand and she walked between the parked cars. I knew I would have killed her. She would have been under the front tire, there were witnesses. One couple came over and offered to give me there names and addresses. The sergeant came to the scène.

I was fucking pissed, not at the girls but, where was the mother. The only thing the boss said, I know he knew I was mad, "Al do your job", I calmed down. We went to where the mother lived, my partner and I. We knocked on the door she came to the door with some fucking guy, doing drugs, or drunk as a skunk, he had no shirt on. We left. In this precinct you can make a lock up any time anywhere. Hey there's only so much you can do. I don't know, maybe, making excuses, or just tired of this shit.

It wasn't right after this accident, but maybe, soon after. The department set up a new thing, called the Accident Review Board. After I guess, a certain number of accidents you had, you had to go in front of this board. The board was there for, either, leave him in the car or take him or her out of the car for a certain amount of time.

From what a cop that was working there said, I think I was the first cop to go in front this board. When they called me in, I was sitting, I think in front of a Chief, or an Inspector, a D.I. on my right and I think two lieutenants on my left.

The Chief or Inspector that was sitting at the desk and looking at a folder. He says "you know you had six R.M.P. accidents since you're on the job", how many did you have with your private car, "I said "I think about six", he tells me "I don't think you're a good driver", I tell him "everyone's entitled to their own opinion, but I don't agree, I think I'm a good driver". That was it. I went back to the precinct. The desk officer said that he got a phone call, and they said to put you back in the car. Good to have friends in high places. Or I said the right thing. I knew the D.I. when he was the Captain of one of the precincts I worked in long before this one.

The same cop with the accident on Eastern Parkway, he was an ex C.O.,{ Correction Officer], who I met some time later running at Long Beach, on Long Island, he said he made lieutenant.]We made a gun collar. He took the collar, and he wrote it up, meaning, for a medal, sometime later he gets the paperwork back, and tells me. "Remember that medal for the gun collar I wrote up, we got an Atta boy", I said," what's as Atta boy", he says," it a pat on the back", I said." Hey I never got one of those", I laughed, one of the few times I ever laugh. A couple of days later, I'm walking out of the precinct by the back door and into the parking lot, my head was down. I felt a pat on the back, it was the lieutenant I liked, and he gave me an Atta boy. First real one I've ever gotten, I'm sure he meant it.

Another time, we're riding; we get a call to see a complainant. We go to Franking Avenue and Park. The job was on Park. We go into the building, knock on the door, a woman answers. This one was a working class mother with two children, no father. She tells us a story. About a guy, who was a bum, he lived in the boiler room of the building in which she was living. She said, he would climb through the back window, while the children were at home and she was at work, he would go through the house, then leave, a little hard to believe. The windows had no locks, we took a report. We went to the back of the apartment building, banged on the door, no answer. Referred to the detectives.

I heard nothing about it, until I read in the papers. This bum climbed into the apartment through the back window. I don't remember which child he killed, the boy or the girl, and seriously wounded the other. It took me a while to get over that. I used to wake up in cold sweats, if we only got him that day. I put it to rest that it wasn't my fault. You always feel like you could have done more. I still think about it.

I'm doing a late tour. We get a call possible child abuse in an apartment, meet complainant outside. We get there and see this guy waiting outside.

He tells us his mother is taking care of his two boys and he thinks one of them is being abused. I guess he didn't want to confront his mother, being; he probably needed her to take care of his kids while he was probably at work. We go to the apartment. A woman answers the door, we tell her what we're here for, and she lets us in. We talk to her, and say we want to see the children, she shows us the two boys. One was and looked very healthy the other boy looked like he was being starved to death. I 10-85 the sergeant, to meet us at the location.

When he comes in and sees the boys he tells us to call a bus, [ambulance]. The bus takes them to the hospital, what hospital, I don't remember. We meet the bus at the hospital; they take the kids in. the sergeant meets us there. We are in one of the rooms waiting with the boss, this nurse comes in and starts screaming at me how can you do this accusing her of abuse on and on and on, I turned around, I look and the boss. I said," Hey serge I'm not in the mood for this can you take care of her", he gets up and talks to her. I went back to my partner. He was the boss of the Buddy Boys, the late tour boss. Double edge blade nice guy. Probably hit a raw nerve with the nurse, or she had a flash back of her own life.

Another time I'm doing a day tour, driving down St John's Place, I was the recorder. I see on one of the corners a crowd, it was S.O.P. {standard operating procedure} for most of the cops I worked with to drive on by, I said most, not all. This one I had to tell him to stop the car. I get out, cross the street. I see a tall thin boy hands up and against the brick wall of the building. He had no shirt on and this woman with what look like an extension cord was whipping his back. His friends or the crowd cheering her on, I stopped her. I said," What are you doing". She tells me her father did it to her and I'm doing it to him, her son. I tell her," this is wrong, you can't do this" She puts her head down and meekly walks away. I guess some people have to be told that some things are wrong, she could have been arrested, and that's where common sense comes into play. If you don't know you don't know, sometimes someone has to tell you the difference between right and wrong. You're brought up with it and you think its right.

The three times I was in the emergency operating room was when P.O. Brown was shot and killed. This police officer, who at the time he was killed. There was snow and ice on the ground. He was coming from a building walking in the street; he slipped and fell into a parked car. The owner got out started arguing with him and then shot him, also in the operating room, there were plainclothes O.C.C.B. cops [organize crime control bureau] and I'm sure it was the same Chief who asked me on my foot post what am I doing. Protecting and something else.

The other time I was in the operating room, is when this small Albino guy, cut this guy with a razor. We put the guy that was cut in the R.M.P. After talking to him in the car, I saw that his intestines were hanging out. We got to the hospital, I told the staff what I had, they started moving like there was no tomorrow. I went in with them, he was drunk and making a big stink, they were unable to do anything, so I leaned over and whispered to him," if you don't make them help, you're going to die", that quieted him down. Maybe, words of wisdom.

The other time is when we received a radio run man shot. We found him on the side walk, laying face up. A small hole in the front of his head, exit wound from the back of his head, with some brains hanging out. We followed the ambulance to the hospital I go into the emergency operating room, there's doctors and nurses, and he's on the operating table. There looking around, nodding, they looked at me, I nod too. I'm sure we were all on the same wave length; you know brains hanging out, machine, and brain dead. Or just let him go. It was probably drugs or robbery, because he had new sneakers, dungarees and shit.

I guess I was there for some time and tired of listening to the bullshit, it was a day tour and I walked into the precinct, either late morning or early afternoon. The door to the muster room was closed and. I said "what's going on" they said Community meeting. So I open the door and walked in. The D.I., the one who was called back in from retirement, was talking. So I'm listening, in the back there's the black detective. The one whom I told he was show boating on a back-up, the time we received the gun run and he showed up with the State Senator, the same guy who pick me up on St. Johns Place when I was assaulted.

Well anyway, I'm listening, the D.I. is looking at me, because, either I'm picking up vibes from the people that were there, or it was me, because I'm saying to myself what bullshit. So he's looking and I think he's getting the impression that I'm going to say something, he looks at the detective and I mean looks, so the detective walked me out of the room, before I opened my mouth, and put my foot in it. I'm sure even after that he still liked me. Some people are diplomats, some run at the mouth.

The other time I was in the muster room, I'm listening the some of the big wigs of the P.B.A., talk. They're handing out pamphlets and papers, so I tell them instead of handing out all of this crap, why don't you put the money and try to get us a better raise. I remember in a few precincts they wanted me to run for P.B.A. delegate. I would have like to run in this one, but I didn't have the balls because of the fear or the embarrassment of not getting any votes. Added, no big deal, when I lived on Long Island, I ran for office with the State and School Board, my wife at the time didn't even come out and vote for me. So I guess after the precinct's P.B.A. thoughts, it just prepared me for her shit.

I hooked up with another guy, before he became one of the stars in the book Buddy Boys. Real nice guy, soft spoken, good cop, street smart, we worked together for about nine months. His big love was hunting, every season he take off from work, I think it was for two weeks in November and go deer hunting. Then there was black powder season, where the only rifle you could use was a black powder, and how he would dress up in deer skin, you know, the Davey Crocket style, yea he had a big love for hunting.

My wife and I went over to his house for dinner one night. He lived in Valley Stream, we had dinner. He had one daughter at the time, he always talked about her, you knew he loved her, I got the feeling his wife didn't take a fancy to me, I think because we were getting close. Just my feelings. She wasn't too much of a talker.

One time we did a four by twelve, I ask my wife if she could cook dinner, we were going to come home for meal. She made stuff Cornish hens, nice spread; she was always that way, not to impress anyone she just liked to cook. She liked him; she liked the way he spoke and his manner. We kept the radio on, what else is new; it was like a third ear. When we finished dinner, we stood up said cheese and she took a picture of us together, as of today this might be the only picture I have of myself in uniform. Then we went back on patrol.

He talked about himself and his father, if I remember correct they were very close, and how his father always lied, and he guessed that's why he lies so much. I just listened.

We were driving down Fulton, we see this guy with aluminum foil in his hand with something wrapped inside. We stopped him, "what do you have in your hand?" we take it and open it up, in it was something dark brown and soft, "what's this?" "That's incense man", he smells it, I smell it, smelled sweet. We took a piece; threw it on the top of the dash, you know give the car a fresher smell. We found out later we're driving around with harsh on the dash. No wonder why we were getting hungry. Live and learn, we laugh about that one.

In the basement of the precinct there was a bench and weights, when I first got there, on meal, instead of eating, I would work out. From there, it snowballed into a few more guys showing up. Then we chipped in for weights and a machine. This one police officer, who was transferred from another precinct to the 77 precinct. He built this huge room; I'm talking a room, door, framing, walls. I don't know if it's still a weight room.

I used to tell the guys, rather than drinking, I'd work off the stress by lifting weights. It turned out to be a nice gym, no air conditioning, just a fan. When meal came I'd go to the gym, my partner, he would take the car, tell me he'd picked me up later, I said o.k. I remember one guy coming into the weight room sitting down saying, "yea, Al, I got to come in and start working out" as he's sitting their swallowing down a beer. I thought that was funny. He was to be my ex partner's partner later on, the other half of Buddy Boys. Nice friendly guy, most of the guys in the precinct liked him.

We were on Nostrand Avenue. We went into this place that was doing numbers. The owner came out, a real dapper and talker. We tossed him; he was trying to sweet talk us out of locking him up. We took him to the precinct and gave him a D.A.T. [desk appearance ticket] which was at a later date; he would have to appear in court. We met him a few more times, we used to stop and talk to him. He said he had two places like the one that we busted him in. He was always in a suit, real ladies man, always up and happy.

We saw him another time, he seem very nervous, he told us about this guy that was, was after him. At first he wanted us to stake out his place. Hang out in the back, to get this guy. Then he'd say, this guy was wanted by the police, and that he said," If any cop came after him he would kill them", I got the feeling he wanted us to kill him. We started walking away, he started double talking, reading between the lines, I told my partner he just offered us five hundred dollars to kill that guy, after that I knew this guy was after him. About two weeks later, he, the one that told us about the bad guy, was killed on, I think, Bedford Avenue and Fulton. Prices, five hundred for a kill, three dollars for, half chicken and rice, plenty of hot sauce, go figure.

When I first got to this precinct, every person I met or talked to on the outside, gave me the impression that every cop was dirty and that all R.M.P.s were there personal car service. And that a lot of people who lived in the area, were so distraught and fed up with their lives. It seem like they were afraid to kill themselves. So they would want us to do it for them, by doing

something crazy or intentional, and putting us in a position, that we can take their lives. If you're paying attention, little by little, you start figuring things out; I used to call that suicide by cop. And if you're not paying attention, you just might be their angel of death.

TAKING IT OFF TRACK,
A BIT OF INFORMATION

My partner, one from Buddy Boys. His wife had another daughter. You could tell he was a proud father, I had no kids at the time. He was always talking about his daughters. We made collars. One time he told me, he knew of an ambulance team that was stealing and selling hypodermic syringes to the drug addicts. We went into a place, moved a refrigerator and behind it were a box of needles.

When I had a foot post on St. Johns there was a Methadone clinic where the drug addicts used to get there Meth from. Methadone was given to a heroin addict, trying to get you off heroin. I'm going back and forth with my writing., I was still a young cop still learning and hopefully will learn for the rest of my life. I remember one of the drug addicts I was talking to and educating me. She was teaching me on how to read a methadone bottle. She said if it was more than this much in it, the person who had it, they either stole it or robbed it from another person. She showed me the bottle she had, was more than the approved mark, than she got scared, she saw my eyes, I figured she thought I was going to lock her up. I said," thanks" and walked away.

Next time I saw her, I got a big hug. Another street lesson. We soon started to break the drug dealers' balls. We stopped this guy who was walking down one of the streets, he had with him, leather, what looked like a shaving case, we opened it. He had a wad of cash in the case, around six thousand dollars; we knew it was dirty money, singles, fives and tens. We called the sergeant to the scene. We asked him how we can take the money from this guy. The sergeant knew of a law, where if we thought it was drug money, because we were in a drug location we could voucher it for safe keeping, and if he bought down a receipt that he got the money from a legitimate source, he could have it back, something to that effect. It made our day. You knew it was drug money we vouchered it and gave him a receipt.

Another time we chased this guy into a building, up two flights of stairs to the third floor. There's this door in the hall towards the back of the building. I was always cautious about going through doors so we didn't run through it. We opened the door, the only thing that was there, was the door; it dropped two stories down into the back yard. The police department always warned us about booby traps. They said the Rastafarians or Jamaicans were good carpenters and they would make traps, or hidden compartments in the walls, so if you tossed them and they were directing you to a certain wall to lean on, there might be a dropout in the wall with a gun in it, all fits.

We grabbed some guy at another drug location. He was sitting on a motorcycle. We took him in, for loitering with the intensions of buying drugs. He tells us, he's an informant for the police department. A biker type; he gives me a code word. So I make a call to Intelligence, I spoke to a police officer, I tell him what we have, I give him the code word, he hands the phone over to a lieutenant. The lieutenant says," yea he did some work for us, but not for some time", he says do what you want. We cut him a break.

My partner told me about his brother-in-law and what he did. I think he worked in the 75 precinct. He was in Anti Crime, and things were happening in his unit and how he went to I.A.D. I don't remember if he said he wore a wire. His brother-law—would talk to him. He sounded like he was proud of what his brother-in-law did and almost wishing he could do something like that. I had the feeling that he was thinking about going into I.A.D. at that time. You could tell by the way he was talking he would have been proud to have done that. At that time you knew where his head was at. Still to this day, that's how I want to remember him as the good guy, the street smart cop, the go getter. With him, it was speaking softly and carry a big stick.

P.S. Our specialty was half chicken and fried rice and plenty of hot sauce. We'd eat that almost all the time for meal.

We were doing a day tour, when we get a 10-2, come back to the precinct. When we got there, there was a photographer from Newsday waiting for us. The desk officer told us, he wanted to go to a certain area of the precinct, and a certain block. The photographer wanted to take pictures of the two of us patrolling that block on foot. That block, was where a little girl was killed, the day before.

But, before that call to come to the house, myself and my partner was at a building, talking to some of the tenants. They had no electric and heat for two weeks. I told them that we do something about it. You know start making calls to certain companies. After that the call came, go to the precinct. What luck a person from Newsday. He wanted to go to the spot where the girl was killed. I told him before we go there; I'd like to show him the building where the tenants were freezing. I knew by the look on his face and my partners, that they didn't like the idea. We went anyway. He looks around and said he would do something. Then we took him to the other location.

We got out of the R.M.P. on the corner of the block and pretended to be on foot patrol, walking down the block, myself and my partner, he started taking pictures. Then we drove him back to the precinct. I went home and told my wife that I was going to be in the papers tomorrow. When the next day came, we got the paper, he did something alright, and he cut me out of the photo. I told her you know the way it is, they like to see tall cops in a picture, which looks a lot better. He did nothing about the building with the no heat and electric. I still remember his name.

Myself and my partner got along good as a team and I like him as a friend, for some reason down the road, the stories he was telling me didn't mix and I knew he was lying to me. So I came into the precinct one day and told him we should split, I knew he was surprised, I just told him it wasn't working out. That was it. I went back to bouncing around. I knew we were still friends. I learned after awhile from being married that lying is part of a relationship, but the two parties have to do it, not just one.

Every time he was out there, I always backed him up, and he did the same. A lot of times when something was wrong or going down, he would 10—85 my sector [needs a back-up]; once he thought this guy in a certain car was selling guns. He 10—85 me, we did a car stop, nothing, better safe than sorry.

He called me down at one of the Mosque, on Herkerimer Street. I had dealings with them before. It was no big thing, but respect is respect. I'm working with another guy passing this Mosque. This Muslim that was sitting in front of the building, starts pointing and laughing at us, I guess it was one time I took it personally. I stopped the car; I told him let me tell you," I know you don't believe in our laws, but when we come around you show respect." Then the head guy comes out, I told him what had happened. He looked at this guy and I mean, this guy cowers and goes back into the Mosque, he apologized, it won't happen again.

So my ex partner calls my sector down, what happened was, these Muslims caught this guy pissing on their sidewalk, and they keep the street and sidewalk clean. When I get there, these Muslims, around twenty or plus, are dressed if full camouflage uniforms. They were in the street with what looked like single bolt action rifles, the rifles were white. We assumed they were ceremonial weapons. Well they were going to take care of this guy, and I mean, he was terrified. I remembered the head or leader and I told him it was our job and we'll take care of it. He looked at me, I'm sure he remembered me. They let him go.

Now we're all walking back to the R.M.P.'s, the two sectors police officers, when all of a sudden, the group that was in the street, they all started screaming, as if they were going to charge. The other guys looked back, I kept waking. Because I knew the head guy gave us his word. These little things make your day.

The Fulton Street Mall. The security guards in that mall were armed with 9mm hand guns. I was passing by, when I see my ex partner in a heated argument with one of the security guys, neither of them were backing down, I didn't know what it was about. We stopped the car, I get out, I go, as a go between, and for some reason they both bow out gracefully. When the security guard walked away, my ex, said," thanks Al". I knew he meant it. [My ex, I fell like I'm talking about my wife]

Me, like I said I would rather talk than fight, don't get me wrong, if it came to push and shove, no problem, if I could talk my way out of a situation, or calm a situation with words, I'd do it. My last resort was violence. I used o tell my wife," I could talk the balls off a bull". Now I get tongue tied if I speak more than ten words. I guess, I'm all talked out, I hope not.

P.S. He had a foot post. I didn't realize it at the time, he said, "Al, if I were to go to hell, I'd take you with me, because I know I get back". Every once in a while, I think it was my fault, he went off the road, because I split with him, but then, I figured, we make our own call.

I would always wonder whatever happened to him. I heard his wife left him, for some reason, probably the pressure of what he was going through when he was caught. I think deep down I needed some closure. This is the story I got. I'm on Merrick Road in Valley Stream, in an accessory auto parts store. I started talking to the guy behind the counter, he walked with a limp. I told him I'm, a cop, he said, he was a cop on three quarters; he said he worked in Brooklyn North. I said yea, I worked in the 77 precinct, my ex partners name came up. Now this is what he tells me, "yea his brother came in the other day", I didn't remember him telling me he had a brother, he said yea, "they found him hanged in one of his relatives closets", if it's true, small world, closure. I take everything with a grain of salt, especially with no proof.

One time he stopped me on a corner while he had a foot post, and wanted to talk to me, he said he was in big trouble, and he had to talk to someone, I mean he was very nervous, I told him to talk to a psychiatrist, to get it off his chest for confidentiality. Another time at the precinct we were in the locker room alone. He gave me a tape recorder and a wire, he said, to hold this until he ask for it back, he thought someone was going to check his locker, and I also thought he was doing what he wanted to do. I held it a couple of days then he asked for it back. I knew he was scared.

I was working in the 112 precinct when the 77 scandal broke. I heard about him and his partner, I called his house, I knew that the voice on the answering machine didn't sound like him; I thought it might be I.A.D., but I left a message anyway. I said, if you need a back up, or you think anyone is going to try to kill you, let me know and I'll drive you, then hung up, I don't remember if he returned my call. When I retired, I became of personal body guard, and body guard business, "ESCORTS", so again two and two does make four.

I bounced around a little more, than hooked up with a female cop. I think, but, I'm not sure, that we were the first male, female R.M.P. radio team in the precinct.

We had a few incidents. There's, one, we were on Franklin Ave. I don't remember what tour, I'm in the driver's seat, some guy comes up to the radio car, on my side, he says come on out, and he says, he wants to kick the shit out of me, it didn't register, we're having coffee, he said it again, I think after the third time it clicks. I turn to her and say is this guy talking to me, she said yes. So I get out of the car, she follows; I throw him up against the car. He's a big heavy set guy. He starts to tussle; I didn't realize that she called a 10-13, officer needs assistance.

I take out my night stick, I don't think I ever used it before, I usually used my black jack, so I hit him in the head, it bounced off his head and hits me in the forehead, all cars responded. She looked at me; you got some mouse there, that's what you call a knot on the forehead.

Another radio car is going to take the prisoner to the house, I yell, the officer's name, and say; "make sure no one touches him". Because I know what could happen. We go back to the precinct, she takes the collar, she tells me, go to the hospital, I can't look at that anymore. She's referring to the knot on my forehead. Or maybe like my ex, that would say the same thing and she would be referring to me, hahaha. Another cop comes up and says," lose hand", and smiled, loose hand meant I held the nightstick with a loose hand, and that's the reason it bounced off of him and hit me in the head, if must of happened to him or someone else he knew. He would become one of my partners, when his partner has a heart attack. I'll stick with the slapper.

We were, the female police officer and myself, driving down one of the side streets, from Atlantic going towards Fulton. It was a four by twelve tour. She's driving I was the recorder, my window was down. We stopped, waiting for the traffic to move. When some guy comes up to my window from out of nowhere, he says "those two guys in that cab, just rob a guy with a gun", I tell her, "you listen to what I say, follow them", I put it over the air, we're following two guys in a cab, possibly robbery suspects, gun involved." I tell central our location. I start giving Central a blow by blow description of what we're doing. Saying, "we're making a left onto Fulton Ave". There's traffic, the cab's moving slow. I see the guys in the back looking back. I'm telling Central where we are. It looked like they were getting very nervous, so I tell Central we're going to take them on Bedford and Fulton. My partner puts her lights on, we stopped the cab, we both jumped out of the R.M.P., we open the back doors of the cab, guns drawn, as the doors were opening, the cab is now being surrounded, by R.M.P's from about three different precincts. She screams, "Don't move", their hands are up, the guys are all around, I'm talking about the other police officers. We found the gun and jewelry. We take them back to the house, or precinct. She takes the collar.

My old partner, from Buddy Boys, takes me on the side, he says Al," I was just up in the squad room and I'm sure they have the complainant on this robbery", sure as shit, he comes down, the complainant says," that's them". he tells them, he's pissed for waving that gun at him, he says, "I have friends in there", which, is the joint, "and they're going to make you bend over", if you know what I'm saying. She wrote it up for a medal, we got a metal, later on, I received a letter from the District Attorney's Office, it came to the precinct, telling me thanks for a great job, that they got two to six years. We worked together for about three or four months than she split from me. Nothing new, story of my life with woman, hahaha. She ended up doing under cover narcotic buys and getting the shield. It was a pleasure, nice looking girl.

From there I bounced around a lot. They gave me, most of the time, all young cops, male and female to work with. There were some females, who were just like the male cops, who didn't want to work, and they hung out with the guys to show they were part of the crew. And there were others who I would trust with my life. One, she said her and her husband had an antique store in Manhattan, great sense of humor, always laughing big smile, very aware, played the game. Smart girl and sharp, you could tell.

She was on the T.S. or [handling the phone, years ago it was called the telephone switchboard when calls came in, you had all the plug ins, where you plugged in to connect a call. The first time I saw that I worked in Manhattan north precinct] one night, I was in the precinct on meal. She came down to the lunch room, and tells me, she just gets a call from a person. The person tells her, that there's an R.M.P., or the caller said a police car, I think it's breaking into a school and robbing it. She was given the R.M.P. number and tells me who the team was. I know one of the guys, my old partner that I worked with from another precinct. Who's now at this precinct, under a black cloud. I think for the same thing that he was accused of doing now, Burglary. What should she do? She was nervous. I would have been too. I told her make an entry on the sheet, and tell the desk officer. Write it in your memo book, names and time and what you did. Don't know what happened after that. We worked a couple of times together and I knew she had my back. Nice Italian girl.

Another time, the Buddy Boys team does a car stop. They put the plate over the air, it comes back 10-16, stolen, the guy that's in the stolen car, is a uniform cop from one of the precincts. It seems like, he borrowed a car and he put stolen plates on it. He was another cop under a black cloud. The team that stopped the car gave it back as condition corrected, proper ID. Somehow this young sergeant gets involved; he probably responded to the scene, they tell him the story.

I was in the precinct at the time, so I didn't know what was happening. The sergeant comes back to the precinct, he sees me and tells me the story, and tells me who's involved, and what do you think he should do. I told him these guys that stopped the car don't give a shit and they'll take you down. I would go by the book on this one. That's what he did, I.A.D., Duty Captain and paper work. The last time I saw him, he was in the 84 precinct. I don't know if he made lieutenant. But he tells me, they made him the Integrity Control Officer, we could only smile. Sometimes life takes a turn, and puts you in a different position.

Before this happened, we changed precinct commanders, it was said, they ask this D.I. [deputy inspector] out of retirement, and see if he could straighten out the precinct. I had a few dealings with him, nice quite, well reserved man, all the men liked him, except the wise guys, they didn't trust anyone, I wonder why? I asked him if I can get into O.C.C.B. (organized crime control bureau] [he told me that you needed someone to make a phone call, or do you have anyone that could make a phone call. I said no, then said," could you make the call"? He asked me how would I like R.I.P. [robbery enforcement program], I told him "yea".

I ended up getting an interview with O.C.C.B. There were a few other guys at the building I went to, also waiting to be interviewed. I didn't have a clue about interviews, when it was my turn to speak to the Inspector. He hit me with, did you ever smoke pot, I say yea, I coughed a lot, I didn't like it, he said what would happen if someone put a gun to your head, I told him, after that nothing came of it, probably wrong answers. I left.

I'm trying to make this connection between myself and the D.I., about what happened with the event, of the cops with the stolen plate. Well anyway, I'm sitting around in the precinct when I see the D.I. in full dress uniform rushing out of the house, so I run out with him, I thought something happened, because usually he doesn't move that fast. I asked him, "what happened", he says," nothing", I told him, "I saw you moving fast and I thought something happened", he looked, then he left.

So now here's the connection. I'm in the precinct behind the area that's fenced in, near the desk. I was surprised that there was not a desk officer; and no one at the T.S. the precinct looked like it was empty. This happened a short time later, after the incident with the car stop with the police officer, the stolen plates, the sergeant the whole nine yards.

The two cops that were going to be known as the head Buddy Boys came into the area of where I'm standing and it looked like the way they were standing, it look like they were going to draw on me and I got no place to go and my backs up against the wall. Now the D.I. [Bishop] who was in his office, comes running out [I always called him Inspector], with his gun on, now he stands beside me on my left, and him looking like he was ready to draw. These two guys back down fast, eased out of the precinct. I never saw this D.I. ever carry his weapon while in the precinct. He went back into his office without saying a word. I wonder if I'm in over my head. Well that day I believe the D.I. saved my life. What could have happened, and this is a maybe, no one in the precinct, they could have said Al flipped, he drew his gun, pointed it at us, and we had to shoot. Thank you, I'll use the word Inspector, but things happen so fast and sometimes I miss a cue. Sometimes the cue could mean life or death.

From Vanderbilt Ave in Brooklyn, we moved to Queens. We bought a co-op, in Little Neck. So I started to take the Interboro Parkway to work. I was doing a late tour, driving down Athletic Avenue; I think I was in the 75 precinct when I see this guy on the opposite side of Atlantic Avenue. This guy looked like Charles Manson, bugged eyes long hair, beard, grimy. He's walking fast, and looks like he's after a woman carrying a baby; she was looking over her shoulder, with a terrified look on her face. I stopped the car in the middle of Atlantic Avenue, I jumped out of the car, gun in hand, I crossed over the other side of Atlantic, I point the gun, they stopped and, they look. I tell them I'm a police officer she tells me, everything's alright, everything's alright. You could have fooled me. I arrived at the precinct late. I told the desk officer, who again was this lieutenant I liked. I thought someone was going to be assaulted, so I checked it out. He looked, put his head down, I went downstairs to dress.

There was this club on Vanderbilt Avenue. I didn't get the job or go there; there must have been a dispute. So a few R.M.P's responded. They all went into the club, after it was over, they came out to their cars and found that all the tires on the cars were slashed. That's the type of respect you got from that precinct. A few guys started to wall paper the block, I never heard if they got any results.

I was off duty driving with my wife, going from Long Island to Brooklyn, to a costume party. I'm dress as Dracula, my wife as a cat. We were on the Belt Parkway. There wasn't too much traffic. We were in the right lane. Ahead of us was a station wagon, in the far left lane by the guard rail. I'm about maybe 20 feet behind. I'm watching their car, gut feeling. Something tells me, something is going to happen, so I start slowing down. Just under the underpass, the driver hits the guard rail; the car flips over on its top. We stopped. I threw on my flashers, thank God there was almost no traffic behind us, we get out of the car, and two or three people crawl out the windows. there's smoke coming out of the car, people start coming, the driver was stuck in the car, because of his seat belt, I crawled into the car, can't get the seat belt lose, another guy crawls in, gets him free.

Radio cars are on the scene. I recognized one of the sergeants that used to work with from the 61 precinct, many moons ago. He doesn't recognize me, maybe account of the custom, or maybe of the years that passed. I tell him I worked at the 77 precinct, he asks me for my name. I told my wife," get that guy that unhooked the driver from the car". He was gone from the scene, he was with, and I think his girl friend. He came back, I told him to give the sergeant your name and telephone number and that he was involved also. After this, I left for the party.

A while later, maybe a couple of weeks passed. My friend who is the inside man, he looked like he was beaming at me, he tells me," there was this phone call from a sergeant and he wanted to put you in for a Civilian Commendation", so he gave the phone call to the desk officer. The desk officer told him that I was a police officer. He said he wanted you to give him a call. I called him. I guess I forgot to tell him I was a cop. He says he wants to write it up, is that ok; I said sure, I never heard anything after that. Thank God it wasn't day time." Sun, Dracula" oh well.

Another time I was in the precinct parking lot, just standing there. When these two gold shields in uniform come in, one black cop, one white cop. The black cop stands facing me, like we're going to have a shootout, his hands up and around his gun, I stand there just staring at him, I can see he's starting to move around, and getting very nervous. Then he starts yelling, it's not me, it's him you want, it's him you want. It was like he flipped. The guy he pointed to, was leaning on the gas pump, couldn't see if his hand was on his gun, but it did look like it from where I stood, maybe another Al flipped deal. I knew he was dirty, this from a reliable source. He and his partner were shaking down drug dealers. Again who do they think I am I.A.D. I had the feeling that ever since I got into that precinct they either though I was F.I.A.U., OR, I.A.D.

Let me tell you something I'm not slow; sometimes the cat does catch up to the mouse. I just didn't want to admit it? I don't remember who I told; it could have been my old partner before he took a turn. But looking at the crew. I said most of these guys were followers, and if the shit hit the fan, they would give each other up in a minute. There was maybe one or two that you might have to be careful with. I know I was invited to do steady late tours by this one boss. But I told him I hated late tours, no more said.

I rode with this one cop, transferred in from a different precinct, again, under a black cloud. I rode with him a few times heavy set, good street cop. We're driving down Eastern Parkway, lights and siren. I think it might have been, investigate sniper on a roof. He's driving, as he's driving, he's looking in the rear view mirror and combing his hair. I started smiling; I guess can never be too neat, oh you know with the sniper. When we got to the scene or address, as we were going up the stairs, a foot cop had one in custody and a rifle in hand.

I rode with him again he tells me he was looking for this certain car, it was either a Firebird or Camero, stolen car, weapons, and possibly wanted for rape. If we find it, do you want the collar? "Yea I'll take it". We were driving around, low and behold, we spotted the car.

Now we get into this chase, he's driving; I'm calling it in, and calling directions. These guys are moving. As we're going down this block, at the end near the corner, an R.M.P. is going to road block. This guy is not stopping. The driver of the R.M.P., either he was in reverse or he threw it in reverse. It would have been head on collision. The perps makes a left turn, we're still behind. From there, the perps car starts bouncing off of a few parked cars. I hear the sergeant; he tries to call it off. But we're in the moment.

This station wagon drives across the intersection. The perps car, hits the station wagon in the rear. You can see the station wagon spin around, the perps' car, the whole front is crushed, and then he smacks into the curb. We both jump out. Three perps jump out of the car, one through the window. One perp is ahead of the other two; we're running after them, my partner commandeers a car, now he's chasing the first guy. As he went by, I could have sworn my partner waved. Now, I'm chasing these other two. They go between two parked cars and there crouching as if they have a gun or loading a gun. I'm running with my gun in my hand. This guy I recognized from the neighborhood he's waving and yelling clear the street, clear the street, this guy that was yelling clear the street, his father was a Reverend, who killed two white girls in upstate New York.

These guys get from behind the car into the street. I throw a shot over their heads. They start running again. Radio cars are still coming. I'm getting tired, now I'm on the avenue, they split up I'm going for the one who turned right. I recognized the radio car, I yell into the radio, the police officers name who was driving the car, the R.M.P. is coming in the opposite direction of the perp who I was chasing, he was coming towards him, I yell into the radio, get that fucking guy, I'm getting tired, wasn't the first time I was speaking French, he passes me and the perp. This perp is tired, he stops, puts his hands up against a fence. I came up to him and hit in the head with my fist, just to take out whatever steam in had left in him. We got all three who ran.

We brought them back to the scene, there was still one guy left in the car, he couldn't get out the other police officers had him. We recovered a gun. The sergeant was there, he tells me, the one that tried to call it off." Now what would have happened if you got hurt, what about your wife"? I tell him, "not now serge".

When we got them to the precinct, the one kid that I grabbed said," would you have really shot me", I said" no". This was my collar. Now, my partner wants the collar. He starts telling me, he needs the money; he has mortgage payments, bills etc. I told him, if you're not jerking me around, take it. He took the collar. All in a good days work. This would have been a good write up, didn't even think of it.

Same guy, I worked with that day. I think he did three years in jail, when they got the Buddy Boys crowd. He was another good street cop. Shit happens and people turn, shame.

Some years later, I was in church, in Oceanside, Long Island, where I used to live. I'm standing against the wall of the church. He came in with, I'll assume, was his wife, I spotted him. He's standing in back. When the Mass was over I started walking out of the church. He sees me, I look at him, shake his hand. Say" nice seeing you". Last time I ever saw him.

There was this police officer, Italian guy, and big mouth. I sized him up, as, he had a big heart, every time he would see me, he'd say, "fuck you", I'd smile and walk away. If you rode with him, he'd tell you I'm not doing a fucking thing. I don't give a fuck, and he wouldn't do anything. I began talking to him. He said he was in highway and got burned,.so that's the way it was

He was riding with this one cop; I rode with this cop once before, black guy, big on police brutality. I think he said he was from Corrections. So this Italian cop I'm talking about, was riding with him and something happened. Maybe a week or more goes by. Like I said that was the extent of my conversation with the fuck you Italian cop.

I see he's different he's changed, I saw him in this waiting room, where they dispense gas from, outside the precinct. I see he's not himself, he looks very nervous; I go inside the waiting room. I say what's wrong {name} he looks at me, I see he's scared, I say what wrong[name] I say[name]you got to tell someone, he says." Al, I don't believe it." "I'm riding with that cop" this is the cop I mentioned, from Corrections, he says, "I'm driving, he tells me to stop here and pull over. He gets out of the car, goes into this place. Then he comes running out, throws a bag onto the dashboard. He tells me to go." this guy (the correction cop) just robbed the place and he wants to split up the money. I don't believe it." "I said no way. I go home I couldn't sleep;" "I'm thinking is it a test or what. It was around. I don't remember, if it was two or three days, I was scared," he said, "I called I.A.D., [internal affairs division] they came to the precinct and locked him up." he mentions to me that this cop threatened his family.

I went down into the locker room and I see his locker turned upside down. The cool cops in the precinct turned over his locker, I'm talking about the good guy, the one that went to I.A.D. That annoyed me, they're sending a message. So they took him off the street and kept him in the squad room. I went up to see him soon after, with this young kid I was working with, I took a stand, I said it out loud "you fuck with [his name] you fuck with Al Cimino", the young cop I was riding with said "you fuck with me too".

That kid ended up in S.N.U., [street narcotics unit].one sergeant he was behind the desk, asked me if I wanted to go to S.N.U., I turned it down. It was all numbers; I couldn't stand the numbers, and all of the paperwork.

The last time I saw the cop that did the robbery was in the Supreme Court building, on the second floor leaning over the balcony. He saw me I said hello, than left.

It was a day tour and today we had unit training. It's a class where a police officer instructs us on how a certain procedure is done or new information that the department wants to impart on us. Or an, how to do it class. This was about violent family disputes. Where one person does or physically hurts or wounds the other with an object or a weapon. After the class we went on patrol.

I was working with one of the Buddy Boys. The first call we get was a violent family dispute. He happens to be my ex-partners, partner. We get there, we see the apartment, next to the apartment that we were supposed to go into, its door was open, and we see a male, a female and a little boy. He says the one that owns that apartment; her husband stabbed her and the little boy. There were puncture wounds on both victims, there was an ambulance coming, she says he's still in the apartment.

We go in, I'm first, guns drawn, like I said, I'm very cautious and I'm moving slow, not knowing if someone is going to jump out of somewhere. I respond better that way, so we're moving, my partner, behind. I always tell the person I'm working with to give me some room when they're walking behind me, this way, if I have to move back or jump back there's enough room to do what has to be done. When we go into the bedroom; we see him, he's sitting on the front edge of the bed. I see his face and the way his body is sitting, in other words, the pump is out and there was sweat on his face, I asked him, "you ok", he nods. We put the cuffs on, ambulance and backup here, one of the guys finds the weapon, almost exactly like the unit training class. In class if you make a mistake it's okay, here in the real world, not good. Pay attention.

Again, a day tour. As soon as we get into the street 10-01 comes over the radio, call the house, I call the house from a pay phone in the street. I'm talking to an Anti Crime police officer, nice guy, he had his own medallion cab, he came here from O.C.C.B. [organize crime control bureau] he tells me, a robbery went down this morning, he gives me an address. I think they have the complainant and maybe one or two of the perps. He says the guy with the gun is at that address. He goes by the name of T or Tarzan, can you pick him up for us. He says," be careful".

I'm working with a female, the one with the antique store in Manhattan. I asked for a backup. I'm going through the front door, the backup will go through the rear, second or third floor I don't remember, they ended up standing on the fire escape, in the rear of the building, same guys that almost had the head-on collision during that chase that I mentioned, there the one's that threw the car in reverse. We go knocking on the door, this was our first call. It must have been around 7:30 am, no answer. My partner's smart, she down on the stairs taking cover, so I know my back is covered.

So now, in this hall, there's a vase on a table, I knock no answer, I decide go through the door. Looks good on TV. Well, I hit it with my shoulder, I bounced off the door, hit the table, hit the vase, no more vase. My partner held her laugh. So I start banging on the door again. This time a kid opens it; he looks like he just got out of bed. There were about four teens sleeping and groggy. I saw the backup on the fire escape. They start grumbling what you want; there were no adults in the apartment. So causally I say, "Hey who's "T." they all point to the oldest guy. Made that easy, I cuffed him.

We started looking for the weapon; we found bullets, no gun. The mother of the boys came home. She starts yelling, we told her this guy just did a robbery. I think it was her nephew. She calmed down. We gave him to Anti Crime. Knock Knock, who's there, T, T who, T you in court. My partner and her husband were into antiques, One Ming vase down the tubes, or was it the stairs. Watching too many cop programs.

Day tour, different partner, the cop with the car chase. We get a call possible, E.D.P., [emotionally disturbed person] we get to the address. A person tells us, this guy just came into her house; a stranger, he walked through her house and left through the back door. We go to her back yard. We see him, he just climbed a four foot fence and he's about to open the back door of the ground floor apartment, of another house.

I jumped the fence. My partner who is a heavy set guy, he can't get over the fence, my gut feeling is that he's faking it, not because he's afraid, something else. This is the cop that got three years for the Buddy Boy episode. So I called out to this guy. He was tall and thin, but muscular; I would say around six foot to six foot two. He looks at me with a blank stare. I walked up to him, I say, "no way, you're bigger than me", and I turned to walk away, when he turns away and proceeds to the door, I take him down from the back. I throw my arm around his neck, a knife edge of my foot goes to the back of his knee, and down he goes. I got him on his stomach, I'm trying to grab his arms and cuff him. My partner is still trying to get over the fence. This guys a strong guy, thank God, another team, showed up and hops the fence.

One down and cuffed. He tells me he couldn't make it over the fence. I didn't buy it. I wonder if there was a box of donuts there, would he have made it.

Working a four by twelve. We get a 10—85 [back-up] at a social club. There was a police officer there, another nice guy, big Jamaican cop. He tells me, these two girls from Queens, white girls, were raped, and the guy that did it was in this club, an afterhours club, ok. They gave us a description of the perp. We go in, the girls stay out, I'm first to go in, there's a crowd on the dance floor which opens up when they see us come in, some guy, I'm assuming he's the owner, walks up to me.

Now we're in the middle of the dance floor. I tell him, there's no problem with the club. I tell him what the deal is, ok, we start looking around. There's stairs leading to a basement or to where the bathrooms are. I looked through the doorway and down the stairs, I spotted him. Now, it's a narrow staircase. He's the first person at the foot of the stairs and there are other people behind him, there might have been some people on the stairs. I start yelling at the guy behind him, you with the green shirt, takes the perp, I hope, off guard. I go down the stairs, I passed perp, then from behind I grabbed his shirt, and take him down from the rear, I figured if he had a gun, people might get hurt, they asked me if I wanted the collar, I said no.

Don't get me wrong, I'm not telling you that I'm a good street cop. But after a while, common sense and your gut feeling take over. Like four to twelve driving down a street, a dark street, and street pole light was out. I saw this police officer, talking to a guy under a tree, like pitch black. I tell the cop that's driving, to stop the car. I get out, automatically, I get between the cop, who was a rookie and the guy he's talking to. I pulled a gun from this guys front pants waistband. Now the rookie has a gun collar.

When in doubt check it out. Your there to help you fellow cop, here another rookie told me you got to watch out for those fire escapes, when your going up them, you know they're all rusted, so after that, when I started going up them, I held the railings tight, sure as shit the steps gave way on one of them. I was holding on a little tighter, after he told me that, he help . . . a little info goes a long way.

Burglary call. I was doing a twelve by eight tour. Two guys in front of a building, possible a break-in. One guy, his back facing me, he has both hands in his waist length jacket pockets. I come up from behind him, for some reason, I slid both my hands into his jacket pockets, covering both of his hands, in his right hand, we both come out with a gun. I don't know you just get this feeling. No big deal, one under.

The only problem I had with this collar. When I had to go to the Grand Jury? I went there on a day tour. I looked for the room I was supposed to go to, I found it. I'm waiting to be called. When it was my turn, I was sworn in. The A.D.A. on this case, is asking me questions I'm answering, but I'm a little baffled, because I knew they weren't the right questions, I knew this, because after a few gun collars. There's this format that I was used to hearing, and I didn't hear it from this guy. I'm a little confused. After the questioning was over, I step down and waited outside for the results. I'm hanging out near a wall, in a corner, when this A.D.A. comes out and says," they didn't indict", he tells me, "it wasn't my fault", I said, "I know it wasn't my fault, it was your fault". I usually don't get pissed, but I'm pissed, I tell him," you screwed up the case", I guess I was talking a little loud. I hear one cop say," lower and take it easy".

I stopped and go to the head D.A.'s office, I tell the guy in-charge what had happened and I don't want this guy on any of my cases, and I leave. When I get back to the precinct, I guess I was still perturbed, I tell the desk officer what had happened, he tells me, you can go to the fifth floor in the arraignment count house and make a complaint. I didn't know that, but, at least now I know I have an outlet to take care of a certain problem. I said next time. There was never a next time. I'm glad I didn't keep it to myself, now I know.

There was a big thing at this time about how, we called psychos, they were re-classified as E.D.P.'s [emotional disturbed person] and how they were being handled. It was an eight by four shift. Ten thirteen in a housing project, came over the air. Housing police officers need assistance. It might have been on the eighth floor of this high-rise building. I knew, about three or four radio car teams responded, we all took the stairs, I'll assume we took the stairs, because either the elevators weren't working, which was usual or it might have been faster, it took a little longer for some of the police officers to get to the apartment. Some were out of shape, two of us made it in first, the one that made it with me, good cop. The last time I saw him, it was downtown Manhattan, he became a sergeant; also he was not the police officer I was working with.

When we entered the apartment, I saw a housing female police officer; she was up against the wall bent over a little. She said, and she was kicked in the stomach. On the couch, this E.D.P. was on top of the male Housing Police Officer. It looked like the E.D.P. had his hands around the officer's neck and was strangling him. The other police officer that came in with me was there first, trying to break the hold. I jumped on and we both pulled the E. D. P. Off of the housing cop. We got the E.D.P. on the floor; we're trying of cuff him. Other cops entered the apartment. The psycho's legs were kicking, as we're trying to control him. I'm asking the mother for his name, she gives it, and I'm trying to call him, no way, he's out of it. She says he takes medication, one cop ties his feet together because of the kicking, and we cuffed him, and he's restrained.

A housing sergeant and more housing cops come in they took charge, we leave. Sometime later we get a 10-02 forthwith to the station house. The desk officer says," you handled an E.D.P. in the housing project", yes. "Well he died". Like what the fuck. So all who were involved, we have to wait in the precinct. A P.B.A. delegate, one from our precinct and another from the union came in. They were notified to have a P.B.A. lawyer come down, because an A.D.A. from the Brooklyn D.A.'s office is on the way to read us our rights. Nice to be wanted. Isn't that a song?

There's an Inspector from Brooklyn, an Inspector from Housing, as I was passing by in one of the rooms I saw N.Y.P.D. Inspector and the Housing Inspector talking. I just happened to entered, heard their conversation. I told our Inspector, that we did everything by the book; we responded to a 10-13 for Housing Police, they had the E.D.P. job ... Matter of fact this Inspector was the one who interviewed me for O.C.C.B.

All the young cops that were there, they were all nervous, one asked me, how does it look, I told them it was ok. We did nothing wrong, we did our job. I got tired of waiting, so I put my gym clothes on and went to the basement and started to work out. I came up to check every once in a while to see if the A.D.A. was here. When she came in, I was the first to go into the room. Here was the A.D.A. at the desk; I was sitting with the P.B.A. lawyer, in front of the desk to the side, and the bosses from the two departments. She reads me my rights, she asks," do you want to make a statement", I turn to my lawyer, I ask him what do you think, he says I wouldn't say anything. I said, what he says. Then I leave, and then the others went in.

The next, a week or so, myself and another cop. nice guy, very nervous, he was the partner of the other cop that made it in the apartment first. We have to report the Brooklyn D.A.'s office, downtown Brooklyn. They said they'll be a P.B.A. lawyer waiting for us. When we get there, the other cop is a nervous wreck. I tell him, relax, the P.B.A. lawyer came in. I asked him, what's this for? He says, there just want to tie up loose ends and close it out. Again, I go in first, we sit down in front of her desk. She starts questioning me, and asking the questions in an accusing manner. I felt like I had to wake up the P.B.A. lawyer, so I nudged him with my knee,

I said. "I don't like the way she's talking to me", he says something, she says, that's all, I get up and leave. The other police officer goes in, after a short while, we go back to the precinct. Nothing more heard after that. Trying times. The police officer that came down with me ended up having a heart attack down the road. Later on I teamed up with his partner.

We were doing a late tour; T.S. [telephone switchboard] gets a phone call, go to a location possible child abuse. We get the job. We talk to the complainant outside. It's some guy telling us that his mother is taking care of his two sons; he thinks one of the boys is being abused. We go to the apartment. a women answers the door, "can we come in"?, she lets us in," can we see the children", she shows us the boys one was as healthy as an ox, the other boy looked like he was being starved to death, we called down the sergeant, he looks, we call for a bus, we take them down to one of the hospitals. Some nurse comes in and starts screaming at me. How can you accuse this mother of child abuse and keeps going on? I look at the sergeant and say "hey serge, can you take this I'm not in the mood. Maybe the nurse, can related.

Another time we escorted two people from the Department of Social Services to an apartment. Again child abuse. We knock, the door opens, one of the social worker starts yelling and coming on like a storm trooper. I stopped her and tell her, we do it my way or we leave. We go in, three small children in pampers looking healthy. The apartment was empty, except for maybe two mattresses, it smelled and it looked like they were shitting on the floor. We talked, the father said, "you're not taking my kids", young couple, I knew there was going to be trouble, after talking to them and convincing them, I would meet them down at family court and speak up for then. After a while they let us take the kids. Sometimes a lie goes a long way!

I hooked up with this other cop, his partner was the one who went down to the Brooklyn D.A.'s office with me, and had the heart attack. We did a day tour. We were parked on a corner that had a fruit store near; he went into the fruit store. He wanted to get some fruit, I stayed in the car. I'm the recorder.

This big Jamaican stands on the other corner, opposite the car. He starts smiling at me and lights up a joint, and starts smoking, like, fuck you and you're not going to do a fucking thing, or every cop doesn't give a fuck type of attitude. He's standing there just smoking. When my partner comes out, he gets in the car, I said, [partner's name,] "I'm taking that guy", we get out, cross the street. We grabbed him, a little tussle occurs, we throw him against the car. Now he's scared shit. Another guy comes up from behind us; I pushed him out of the way. We take him to the precinct. He has five bags of pot on him.

Now he's in the house, scared shit. He says to me "you put the fear of God in me man", now I thinking this guy is a dealer, so the other guy might have been his bodyguard. I asked a team that I see in the precinct. Good team, I thought, one of them later on, was arrested with the Buddy Boys and I tell them what we had and if they could go back to that location, I gave them what the other guy looked like. To pick him up, be careful he might have a weapon, and he might be this guy's bodyguard. When they came back, nobody was there. About a week later I passed the place where I made the collar; it's a normal day, the guy that I saw, was sweeping the sidewalk.

There were stores that would open up and the only thing they sold were drugs, O.C.C.B. [organize crime control bureau] would come into the precinct and do a raid, make arrests, pad lock the door. Next day it was opened and under new management. I took part in a raid on Fulton, lock up, pad lock, next day back in business. That's what they called the numbers game.

There was one place, cinder blocked wall, small hole in wall, you pass in money, they pass out drugs, one guy had a toilet bowl next to him that worked, and if we tried to break in, he would flush the drugs down the bowl. I went into a building that had a hole punched through the a wall, what you would call a basement wall, if you knelt down and crawled, you could get in, all the houses were attached, and you could almost get from one building at the beginning to end building at the end of the block, some of the buildings were abandoned, sometimes the drug dealers, they would set up booby traps.

My old partner from my rookie's days was transferred to the 77 precinct under a black cloud. Word was they had him and another police officer on camera, burglarizing a store or something. We hook up for a late tour. Grabbed some guy, I don't remember what charge. To make it easy on himself, he's going to give up some cops that are doing [having sex] prostitutes and taking money. I know we have something. I was caught between a rock and a hard place because the sergeant on duty was the boss, of the group called Buddy Boys. He stayed clean, and retired without incident. My partner tells him what the perp wants to do, I'm standing there, and he's looking at me, the boss. I put the dumb face on, got nowhere. It's tough when you don't know who's who, or you know who's who. Tough, uh!

The last collar I made before I put a 57 in [transfer out of the precinct] was for attempted murder, I knew I was getting nowhere, so I decided to transfer out. I transferred to the 112 precinct, not knowing it was the Borough Headquarters and was not ready for that big of a change in police work that was about to come.

I was mentioned a few times in the book Buddy Boys. I remember reading the book sometime around ten years later very depressing. My ex partner of Buddy Boys on one of the stories he covered for me, or left me out, I'm sure I was the one he or they mentioned as squeaky clean. A little bit of information I was called No Nonsense by some of the cops, just as added thought. Made me feel like someone was paying attention, again

When I got there. There were a lot of young cops a few cops I was acquainted with from the 77 precinct, and some old timers. Bosses who came from high crime areas who worked and some who pretended to work. Now the ones that pretended to have worked. They can be the man, and show all the rookies what it's like to be a real cop.

I had a few off duty incidents not much but enough to mention and full up a page. All of them when I was working in the seven-seven precinct except for one . . .

I was out with one of my friends. He was recently divorced and he wanted to go to a club, ok. I'm at this club, at the bar with him and looking around, I notice these two couples, I think one of the guys wives or girlfriend was flirting with another guy, her escort gets up, for some reason I knew something was going to happen

I walked over, he was about to, what I thought smash his drink glass in her face, I was there, I just said "you don't want to do that", he turned and looked at me, he just stopped, I didn't tell him I was a cop. I guess he just needed a new direction, glad I could help.

Another time, same friend. We were at this other dance club, and again I'm just looking, checking out, no big thing. We left. We were driving up Fourth Avenue, he was driving.

I spotted this guy chasing these two other guys. I remembered them from the club I was just in. I told my friend to slow down, we stopped behind them. The one guy is accusing the other two of taking his leather jacket. One of the two moved to a city garbage bin from the street, he took out a beer bottle, cracks it on the can. I tell my friend to move up. My windows down, he has it in a motion to jab it in the guys face that's accusing them. I told him, "you know if you do that, I'm going to have to shoot you'. He just looked at me. Then I heard sirens and before I knew it, we and the three were surrounded. I told the police officers I was an off duty cop. I guess he called the police before he went out and followed these two. We left. My friend said" this is the last time I'll ever go out with you", he said," He can't take it". That was the last time I ever saw him and we were friends for over thirty years. Would I do it again, you bet. Hey some do and some don't. I do.

I was at an I-Hop with my wife and son, the pancake house. We were eating, when we finished. She took my son to the restroom I waited at the table. I was sitting in a booth near the window. This young guy sits down at one of the tables to my left, a two seat table, he's parallel to me. He put his hand in his pocket and an automatic clip falls out. He sees me look, I turned my head. This was around Christmas, one or two days before the holidays. I was working at the Whitestone pound and they, at that time had taken my guns away. I pretended to make nothing of it. When my wife returned from the bathroom I give her a look, lets go now, she's a very stubborn person and has to argue and debate every fucking thing. Why are you looking at me that way and so on, big pain in the fucking ass, at times.

When we get outside of the place, the pay phone was right in view of the table I was sitting at, so he would see me if he looked out the window. We get in the car I knew I had to do something. Usually holiday season is also robbery season . . . so I'm driving around Sunrise Highway, I saw an R.M.P. parked. I pull behind him, get out and tell him what I think might be going down. He radios it in, then leaves.

I forgot that this is Nassau county, I'm thinking I have to go back, there might not be a back-up and there might be an accomplish in the back of the restaurant, so I go to the place, there must have been everyone in God's country there. I pulled into the curb, and hear either a detective or a season cop ask where's the guy who told you this. Before the cop could answer, he's not here; I opened my mouth and said that's me.

I told him I was a cop from Brooklyn. We went into the pancake house. The guy that I spotted wasn't there, he left. The police officer told the manager what happened. You could tell the guy froze and said," thank you very much for your concern". I went back to the car. My wife said," you always give me those eyes," like as usual it's my fault, she can't do any wrong. That's nice when you're perfect. She doesn't ask questions because it would make her look stupid like with the double homicide, questioned me about every fucking little shit but when it came to something important like my life, fuck no questions, probably the N.Y.P.D. insurance policy. Just me venting, a little anger is coming out, divorce is hard.

The other incident was at another I-Hop or pancake house on Long Beach Road. I called it road rage in a parking lot. Myself and my wife just finished eating. We got in our car and we're driving out of the I-Hop parking lot. When we got close to the exit, there was this Mercedes Benz, female driver and another car, going for the same parking space, male driver with wife or girlfriend. There were three other females in the Mercedes, they left the car and went into the restaurant, I guess to get a table. This guy in the car gets out and starts screaming at the woman in the car. I'm telling you, he's going ape shit. Everyone that was standing in the parking lot turned their backs on the situation. When he pulled open the door of the Mercedes and he starts pulling the woman out of the car.

I was just watching before that, really nothing to do, but wait for it to resolve itself.

I knew when he opened the door of the car; I thought it was a little too much, like he really lost it. I got out of the car, my wife stayed, I went over to him, he was standing outside, he looked at me, the only thing I said was, "your over reacting" he looked, walked away went to the street phone and made a call. That was it. The only thing I though he needed, was a way out. All these other people in the lot did exactly nothing. Helping your fellow man, I guess it doesn't apply to your fellow woman.

A little tad bit of information. Once a week I used to see my grandmother, who lived on Ocean Parkway in Brooklyn. We use to sit, talk and have black coffee [espresso]. It was just before I was going to do a four to twelve. So she walked me downstairs from her apartment, she was close to ninety years of age, and she was standing in front of the house near the driveway, I'm about to enter my car, she called me, Allan, I looked back, come here, I see her and a few guys with her . . . So I go back, she says Mr. So and So this is my grandson Allan and this is Mr. So and So. There are maybe two or three other guys around him. I shook his hand, say hello; he looked, than put his head down, looking at the ground. Who do you think it was? It was the head of organized crime, the Don himself. I said nice meeting you, kissed my grandmother goodbye, and left.

I'm thinking there must be F.B.I. all around here taking pictures of him, me my grandmother my car plates, and so on, according to the job you're not supposed to be associated with anyone from that group. Now if I had a photo, I would have two of me.

Me personally I don't think I gave a fuck. Never heard anything about it, so it was no big thing. By the way the first time I met him, was when I was around twelve or thirteen years of age. I was in the driveway of the same house and my father introduced me to him. I remember he had a smile on that time. He always reminded me of an old sing and song man Jimmy Durante, the one that used to closed his acts with something like "good night Mrs. Calabash where ever you are."

Another little bit of information. I was on vacation, still living one block out of the 77 precinct border line. I had a motorcycle. I made plans with these two guys I knew from my old neighborhood where I grew up. They were going to Canada by bike, sleeping bags, sleeping in fields or off the road. So I decided to take a ride with them. All the gear was packed on the back of the bikes.

Years ago I used to smoke pot. I mean my early days and these guys too. I figured we all grew up and had responsibility, so never gave it a second thought. We get into Canada, nice, no problem. Had fun, it was a nice ride. On the way back going through Customs, we were told to pull over, by one of the custom agents. Young kid working with an old timer.

So the three bikes were parked to the side of the Customs Section. The young kid tells us to unpack all of our belongings and open them up. I mean back packs, small bags and sleeping bags. So we started the unpacking, opening things up, real pain in the ass. Like the old saying 20 pounds of shit in a five pound bag. So the old timer was near me, I tell him I'm a New York City Police Officer, he gives me a look, like, hey, he's a young rookie, so, he has to go with the flow. No problem.

I still thought nothing of it, just an inconvenience. I see one of my friends; he's still on his bike. He has one hand in the air, the young kid says what do you have in your hand, he says "nothing," I can see he's holding like a small container, let me see it. In the container he has hash. Smart move, the kids now thinks he's bagged a smuggling ring. Our shit is on the ground. They take my friend into the office.

Now I look at my other friend, he's a postal worker. I tell him," I'll be right back", I go into the office, my friends sitting down, I start talking to the old timer, I tell him." I didn't know he was caring that Shit" can he do something?" He looked at me; he goes and talks to the rookie. The bottom line was, instead of arresting him they gave him a summons.

No rest, not even on vacation. That was the last time I saw those two guys, not even a thank you. Still I like them, ah well. All's well that ends well.

I was riding with this cop who came from either O.C.C.B., or Robbery. He was awarded the Medal of Valor. I rode with him one day, and ask him how he got the medal. He tells me, he was at his desk when he gets this assignment, pick up these bad guys, I don't remember what for. His regular partner was out for the day, so he was assigned another police officer. They go to this location, find the apartment. He said he was on one side of the apartment door, his partner on the other side of the door. They knocked, identified themselves. The door opens up just enough for the barrel of a shotgun to be push through. He said his partner was almost cut in half with the shotgun blast. He throws his partner over his shoulder, runs down a flight of stairs, he said he puts his partner down, he knew he was dead. He said that he grabbed his partners' gun. Runs back to where the apartment door was, and starts shooting with both guns. He was shooting through the walls and door. I think at the end there were two perps dead, and one wounded. Usually when you receive the Medal of Valor, most of the time you were killed in the line of duty. I told him must have been tough.

We rode together a few more times. He used to eat sun flower seeds and throw the shells all over the R.M.P. Used to annoy the shit out of me, but it could have been worse. I remember we get a job. Man with a gun in this apartment, he's on one side of the door I'm on the other side, he says Al, I knew what he meant, I corrected my position, went behind him on his side.

Same police officer. Day tour, we were driving down Franklin Avenue, one of the, if not worst avenues in the precinct, he says that's one of the perps, that was in that shootout that killed his partner. He probably just got out of prison or he's been out, and

I don't remember if he pointed him out. But I felt like he thought that he had to do something, I also felt that he wasn't in the right frame of mind to do whatever, we rode by. When I used to see him, I looked in his eyes and for some reason I felt like he had it with the job.

Same guy, we had a car stop on Washington Avenue, I'm driving he's the recorder, I'm going to give this guy a summons. So this guy comes out of his car, I'm writing the summons in the R.M.P., and he's at my window in my face yelling and talking shit, I tell him to wait he his car, he's still doing the same thing. I've had enough I get out of the car, grab him and throw him against the car, than I took my hands off and backed off, I said not for a summons, walk back to the car, rolled up the window. He wants my name, again yelling he's going to the Captain, the whole nine yards. When I got out of the car my partner was right there. I rolled down the window, gave him the summons and showed him my name tag; I said here's my name. Nothing ever came about, all talk. I'm surprised I even gave him my autograph. I thought I saw some-thing in my partner's eyes. When I got back into the precinct, I knew the lieutenant the desk; I just nonchalantly mentioned I don't think he should be in the street anymore. From my point of view I think he's had it. Just looking out.

He came over to my apartment when I was living in Glen Oaks, in Queens, because he wanted to talk. Either I was doing something wrong, or I didn't know how to respond. We went down to the beach a few times. He did get three quarters. One hell of a guy.

I knew another police officer who received the medal of valor. He worked for the Port Authority Police. He passed away a while ago.

He and a rookie were on patrol in Manhattan, in the Port Authority Terminal. He was not too distant from his partner, when he said, a homeless person came up on his partner took his gun out of his holster, and killed his partner, when he heard the shot, came running up and killed the perp. Bad day. Nice to have known him too. Wayne Konje:

77 PRECINCT

I was doing day tour. As soon as we got out of the precinct, we get a job, See ambulance at a certain location. When we get there, we talked to the attendants. They said, they got a job at this location, when they went up to the apartment There was this person holding a knife, so they decided waited for us, E.D.P. My partner and I went up, there was this guy standing in the kitchen, with a knife, and he looked like he was sharpening it on one of those stones. So I started to try and talk him down. I knew he was listening, I'm talking and talking. It must have been for at least 20 minutes to a half hour when who pops into the apartment, this black cop, he was an F.T.O., [field training officer], I knew him. He worked mostly in the 77. Real nice guy. He said that he was in the 79 precinct when he heard the job come over. He didn't hear anyone backing us up, so he figured he drop by. I told him I've been Talking to this guy and I'm getting tired so he took over, after a while we talked him out of the knife, cuffed him, sent him with the ambulance attendants. Nice to have friends in long distance places. Thanks, later on he made sergeant

I was doing a four by twelve, driving down Fulton Ave, I saw this woman in a Black coat walking with a bag, and she was a white female, around early to mid Fifties. It looked like she didn't belong in this neighborhood. We stopped the car; I asked her where she was heading for. She had no place to live, she said. We put her in the R.M.P., told Central one female, transporting to homeless shelter. I asked her a few questions. When she started talking, the first thing that came to my mind was this woman was a lady, a lady from the start. I picked up a few things for her to eat. We dropped her off at the shelter. I felt bad that we had to leave her in a place like this, but there was no other choice. I said goodbye, than left. Till this day I think about her. You never know who you'll run into that would make a difference in your day. Good luck. Running on hard times.

I was doing a day tour when I saw four teenagers huddled on a stoop; they weren't paying attention, to what was going on around them. Or they would have been looking out for the police. We got out of the car, we stood near the stoop. We didn't say a word, when they looked up they almost shit, we probably blew their heads. They were doing drugs. I told them, either you throw the rest of the drugs away and walk, or you can get arrested. Three decided to walk, one said arrest me. I guess he thought I was bull shitting, so I put the cuffs on, placed him under arrest, again a no no, too late.

When we got to the precinct, I made him call his mother. He said to her, he didn't do anything, He says, here she wants to talk to you. When I got on the phone, she started yelling at me, the lieutenant was behind the desk. I told her to calm down. I told her the story, three of your sons friends walked, your son decided to get arrested, so here he is, she didn't say another word. By the expression on the boys face, I knew when he got home he was in for it. The lieutenant looks up, looked at me and shook his head, smiled, said nothing. Gave the kid a D.A.T., which is a Desk Appearance ticket. Wrong choice, either A or B there's no C.

I remember when I first got to this precinct. I was on a day tour. I walk in the precinct for a break. The doors to the roll-call room shut. These door were huge sliding doors, they opened and closed like an accordion doors. So I go inside of the muster room. The two cops that had the Washington Avenue post, one the F.T.O and his partner, they have this Rastafarian cuff in a chair, there's a line of cops, mostly rookies, or little time on the job, they were standing in a line. One of the cops, that I guess, made the collar was cutting the Rastafarian's dreads off, and each cop in line, would go up, and punch this guy, the two cops looked at me, I said to myself, not for me and walked out I guess that's taking my own stand. After that, that's when one of them said, you got to be careful walking through a door, you can get hit in the face with a two by four. Ah, okay. This is the way you break the young in, when there to young and impressionable to make their own choice. Teaching the young to run before they can walk.

I remember it was a day tour. I was walking a foot post on St. Johns Place. Still new to this precinct, I mean this type of precinct, totally High Crime. When this guy stops, stands in front of me, starts screaming at me and waving his hands up and down. I have no fucking idea what his problem was or what to do. So I let him stand there and scream. This radio car coming down St. Johns, stops, I recognized them from the precinct. I knew they were a good team. They stopped, the recorder, who they called the Colonel, gets out of the car, takes this guy down, puts the cuffs on him, he's yours, he's under. They take me back to the precinct. The colonel writes up the 61 report for dis-con. I'm not used to this, plus not having enough experience with the Penal law. He gave me the report, here sign it. He writes Loud and Tumultuous Behavior was the reason for the arrest. I didn't even know those words existed. I rode with the Colonel a few Times, real nice quite guy, active cop. Later on he made sergeant. Like I said I don't forget.

I was home, my day off. I usually wake up to the radio, the station was WBLS, and it was a Sunday. So I'm lying in bed listening to the station, and I'm listening to this guy talk, like he was on stage. Talking to an audience telling them we have to get the white people we have to kill them, so on and so forth. I couldn't believe it. I was pissed and upset; I had to talk to someone. I called the precinct and asked if the Inspector was in, the person on the T.S. said yes. Great. This was the inspector, [D.I.] whom they called out of retirement to take over the precinct. I got out of bed dressed, drove to the precinct. I looked in, he was sitting at his desk, and his door was always open. I walked in, told him that I wanted to talk to him. I sat down. Told him what I heard. He told me, the Police Department was monitoring that station for awhile, we talked a little then I left. I felt a sign of relief. Always better to be safe than sorry, when in doubt, check it out.

I was doing a day tour, driving down St John's Place; I was the recorder my Window was down. Hot day, I'm looking around, looking at the buildings, I see the top floor of one of the buildings, there's this very young boy leaning out of the window, nobody else is with him. In this area, there's no window guards. I tell my partner to stop. We get out, I tell him to go to that apartment, and I'll stay outside, under the window, figuring if the kid falls, I could try to catch him or at least break his fall. I tell you, the only thing I thought of was, may sound stupid, I always drop the ball, luckily my partner got hold of the person who was watching him. Thank god . . .

Another late tour at Kings County Hospital, again G building sitting in the same Area, as the people the Police brought in, this time it was crowded in this section where I was sitting. So I'm watching and I'm feeling the restlessness, I knew something was going to happen, sure as shit one fight breaks out then everyone starts to fight. I was like walking between the rain drops; hospital police came, set things back in order. You never know.

A day tour, I drove this sergeant to a construction site. There was going to be demonstration there. The sergeant I drove was the young guy that had the trouble with the police officers that were involved with the stolen plates, with the cop from another precinct during that car stop. This was before that happened. So we go there. There's a trailer and outside of the trailer, there were some demonstrators. The guy that was In charge of the demonstration was the same black guy who ran for President, he was stabbed in Bensonhurst. So when the sergeant goes in, I'm standing outside with the demonstrators they're looking at me, I'm looking at them. I forget to tell you they were there because they didn't have enough blacks working on the job, if any.

It was a white guy that owned the construction company, probably from a different neighborhood. He's like a black organized crime in a reverend costume, if you don't get my boys in there'll be trouble, or payoffs.

So I'm looking at them, you know, I have to say something, me personally. Most of them looked like bums from the street. So I tell them, what did he give you guys, two dollars, what for a bottle of wine, what do you thinks going to happen. His guys, I meant the guy in the trailer, they're the ones that are going to get the jobs, and you are the guys who are going to get locked up. You're the fall guys; they dropped like a ton of bricks, in other words. I opened their eyes. Not so tough now.

Sergeant came out. He said, let's go, we left. Don't know what happened after that, you know a deal was made. The guys out side were the fall guys. If it was anything important, his men would have been outside, prepared to be arrested and for the popularity, and for some news coverage.

I worked with this other guy athletic type. He transferred out before the shit hit the fan. He went to Highway. We get a job missing youth. We go to this apartment. The grandmother was there, she was the guardian of the young boy. We're talking, it was a small apartment, she said, he never did this before; he always came home on time. I asked if she had a picture of the boy, when she showed me the picture, the kid looked like a sweet kid, he looks like the type not to be outside by himself. I said to myself he didn't run away. The apartment was cluttered, stuff all over the place, where's his room, I looked under the bed, there he was. We left, let them talked it out. I could see my partner looked impressed. Not bad, just doing your homework. I'm glad we found him; they would have eaten this kid up. A picture speaks a thousand words, if you're listening.

I was riding with the young cop whose only desire was to become a fireman. We were riding down one of the avenues, might have been Kingston Avenue. It was a late tour. He pulls over to the curb, we were just sitting when he saw smoke coming from one of the apartment house roofs. We call it in; we backed the car up, jump out, run to the top floor of the building where the smoke was coming from, started banging on doors to wake up the tenants. We went to the roof, the roof was on fire, we heard the sirens, and firemen came. We went down stairs waited in front of the building. Chief said there were pails of tar on the roof; someone must have tipped them over and started the fire. I rode with this guy a few times and twice we were involved in fires. Hey maybe there telling me something too. Never thought of being a fireman.

Doing another day tour with this police officer, nice guy, talkative, only wanted to hear himself talk. Anytime I tried to say something, it was like I never said a word. So I just listen. I think it was a pick-up job of a burglary in progress. Some guy on the street points to an open window said some guy just climbed through that window. My partner, he's going to climb the stairs; I'm going to climb the fire escape. So I'm on the top floor, on the fire escape and to get to the open window of the apartment that was being burglarized, your would have to climb over the fire escape railing, put your foot on a small ledge, stretch for the window, than pull yourself in. I said to myself if there's a person in there, he would have no trouble, just to push me off the ledge. I called for a back-up. A young cop from Anti-Crime shows up on the fire escape. I tell him what's going on, I tell him, I'm going in, I said [name] if this guy tries to push me out the window, shoot him, not me. I saw his eyes widened. Luckily, I got into the apartment; he must have left through the front door. By the way, my partner was in the wrong building.

Last time I heard about this cop that I worked with, he became a Lieutenant. As for myself, I took the sergeants tests a few times failed it. Then I took it again years later, went to school, read the books, bought tapes to study with. At the time I was going to take the test the N.Y.P.D. postponed the test two or three times. I lost interest.

I was doing a day tour. We were sent to what was called Jewish Hospital. Some type of a construction accident. I went into the hospital. One of the construction crew got four of his fingers cut off, they gave the fingers to me, and they were packed in ice. I went into the ambulance with the fingers plus the person who had lost them, they said, there would be a helicopter waiting for us at Prospect Park, to fly him out, I think that was the 70 precinct. My partner followed. When we entered the park, where the helicopter was supposed to land. After a few minutes we heard the engine, it landed in a certain area. We put the person and the fingers aboard, and off it went. I guess first time for everything. I use to know a Police Officer, who said he was a spotter on the helicopters, you meet all types of people on this job, and jobs they had before they became a police officer, jobs you would never think of.

A day tour again with a different partner. When there's a 10-85 to the Annex. The Annex is like a Satellite precinct to the main house, also, on the second floor of the Annex building, Transit police used to have a command post there. That was to be sometime later when all the police departments joined together and became one.

When we get there. There's a crowd standing outside the building, I don't remember what for. Making all types of noise and threatening gestures. We get out of the car, there's other police officer there from the 77 precinct. I was standing next to the fence, in front of the Annex, just waiting. The Anti-Crime sergeant that I had trouble with, he was in uniform, standing on the upper steps of the building doing nothing, the crowd is getting louder and more restless he's still doing zip, I'm saying to myself something has to be done to take back the building and the street, and put the crowd in check. Soon after, this guy gets in my face and starts yelling and screaming at me. That's it, I grab him and take him down, throw the cuffs on him, your under arrest, his face told me, he was in shock, and he didn't expect this.

I pulled him into the Annex with a cop and the sergeant. The crowd for some reason got their wakeup call and subsided. I'm giving him a dis-con summons, I'm pretty sure the sergeant knew, I did the right thing, he didn't say a word. This guy that I grabbed was scared, he pleaded with me, you should have thought of this before this happened. Soon after, a priest walks in. He told me that he was a nice boy and he's never been in trouble before. Sorry, one summons served, one crowd broken up. I still remember the 66 precinct when the Hasidic Jews they took over the precinct and the police did nothing. I remembered there were pictures in the newspaper of them standing on the precinct roof top waving. Very political. Didn't like that either.

I was asked if I wanted to be the officer that would stay in the office of Boys and Girls High School. The job was, since the school was one of the toughest in the city and there was so much trouble there. I would stay in one of the offices and if anything happened I would be right there, either to take reports or make arrests, or stop a situation from happening. I thought about it, the thought of being cooped up in school all day, was a turn off, so I turned it down. Had flash backs when I went to High School, never liked school.

I used to visit my brother in upstate New York once a year for a week. He lived at a Monastery. Then he got married moved out and lived somewhere else. I visited him just to get away from my world of crime and to clean out and unwind; I guess it was a retreat. This time I visited him at the house he was living with his wife and family. I get there I'm tired, I just drove about six or seven hours I walk through the door, sit down and his wife asks me if I can come to her school tomorrow and talk to some of her students. She worked in a Bose School. This school was for kids who had disciplinary problems. I needed this like I needed a hole in the head; I'm tired and I needed a break from people. So I did it.

The next day I go to school with her, go to her class, I sit down, like when I went to school, her kids walked in, high school kids, some of them, it was like looking at a carbon copy of me when I went to school. So she's talking, I'm listening, she introduces me, as she was talking I'm looking at them, you know trying to read them, so when I started to talk, my Brooklyn talk came out, they just look and stared, bad guys and girls, most wannabes, probably most of them good kids but they just don't know it yet. Some of them started to ask questions, I don't think they expected to see, like hey, this guys a cop, no way. So one of the boys who was playing bad, said you know my father's a cop. I think that's what broke the ice. I started talking about his father and they were all interested about what he and I, the boy had to talk about. Next year, same thing. I need a break . . . . help

Back at the 77 precinct doing a day tour. I was the recorder. We were driving down one of the blocks, I think Lincoln. We're coming up to the corner. Standing on the corner, was a female holding the hand of her little boy must have been three or four years old. I turn around in my seat slightly, I told my partner to stop car. What I saw, was this black dog, this dog had the mange and looked like it was starving, it's crawling on its belly, on all fours, up to the boy, ready to attack, I jumped out of the car with my nightstick, ready to nail him, he took off. The mother had no clue what was happening. There's never a dull moment. This dog had to be desperate. Thank God.

Just too back track a little. When I first got to the 77 precinct, and I had that look on my face, whatever that look is. it was a day tour, I was in the muster room standing again, with that look, I think the look, it was, new cop on the block, what the fuck is going on here, or how the fuck bad is this place and what the fuck am I into and what the fuck am I going to do. This old timer was sitting at a table on limited duty. He said he was shot that's why he was there, he said Al, everything stays the same just the faces change. I understood what he meant, a little sigh of relief. That might have been the only time he talked to me.

I was doing a four by twelve. We get this dispute. We meet a girl outside of the building very attractive. She tells us that she wants to get her clothes out of this apartment, because she's leaving her boyfriend. So I started talking to her. She says that this is not the first time she has tried to leave. Every time she does this, her boyfriend threatens to kill himself, and she ends up staying, he's giving her one major guilt trip. So we go to the apartment and her boyfriend is there, nice looking guy. We go in, tell him she wants her clothes, and he threatens to throw himself out the window. I see her, she's weakening, she going to stay again, I tell her don't worry he's not going to do it, just get your clothes and we'll leave, I tell her, take my word, and I'm going by what I see in the boyfriend's face. She agrees and starts taking her clothes. We're in the, I think kitchen; we're going to the door, suit case and all. All of a sudden, he jumps on the window sill and yells I'm going to jump, it's a big window, she looks terrified, again, I say, he bull shitting, he's still on the sill, and I convinced her to leave. I told her he's playing on your guilt, and that he's not going to jump.

This kitchen window, looking over into an alleyway of the building. We ask her where she wanted to go. When we get her in the car and we're going to take her to where she wants to go. So, as we drive by the alley, both I and my partner look at the same time, and I guess her too. Nobody's on the ground. All in a day's work. We called his bluff. She'll probably be back, guilt travels by phone too.

And I'll repeat what that old timer said from the 77 precinct said, Al remember everything stays the same, only the faces change.

That's was one of maybe four things or verbal sayings that old timers told me that helped me get through tough times.

Al, just do your job, you make the arrests, and let the courts do the rest. You can't help everybody, so pick the ones that really need to be helped, something to that effect. These things that were said helped make the job easier.

THIS PART IS AT THE
WHITESTONE POUND

When the 77 precinct broke out, there were thirteen police officers were suspended. And I was at the pound at the time, on restricted duty. I started seeing some of the police officers who used to work at the 77, start coming to the pound, whom I haven't seen in a while. Almost the whole precinct was transferred to one place or another. I started seeing old faces, coming here some looked at me, shook hands, others just looked.

One guy who did the steady Washington Avenue post with a younger cop, came down, we spoke, and the only thing he said, was Al, I just want to collect my pension, like I had something to do with him not collecting a pension. As I was listening I'm looking around and I saw we were in front the office window of the Lieutenant and the window was open, and he happened to be or was in I.A.D. Don't know if he said it, there as a coincidence, or he made that statement for him to hear, as if I had something to do with the lockups.

After a while you never know what's going through their mind or yours, you start looking over your shoulder good guy or bad guy, doesn't matter. Sometimes being paranoid does help, but too much can really distort reality. Where you begin to need help, I never made it that far, hahahaha. When you and the whole picture, of what you know about in the precinct and the people you're talking to and who they really are, everything fits into place. Pretends to be a sheep in wolves clothing. With this Lieutenant, I think he needed to be put away, and maybe I needed the room next to his. :]

77 PRECINCT

I was doing a day tour, this just to let you know who your friends are, we get a dispute in a lobby, so we try to break it up and they keep yelling, so I put something over the air. I know we didn't ask for a back-up, who pops by these two Italian guys, good team, sharp cops, [the ones that made the Christmas dinner] I look at them, they said we figured we pass by, we heard your voice change over the air, so we figured there might be trouble. Thanks guys. Good memories, from a whole lot of bad. And from the beginning, when first coming to this precinct from a cop," I like you, so I'll back you up", from famous quotes.

I remember when I got my ear pierced; that was a big thing. The girls weren't allowed to wear hanging earrings, and now a guy with an earring. I wore a black pearl. Soon after that some of the guys started getting there's done. I used to wear this thick lamb skin fur coat and carry a man's hand bag, I drove at the time a 280 Z with the earring, and the guys probably thought it was a tossup. Maybe he is, maybe he's not. They would just look and smile; they never said anything to me. I guess after a while I just did. I never talk about women because I was married, so you can guess. Small bit or personal Information, and filling up the pages.

It was an eight by four, we handled a traffic accident, when we get there, we stopped the car, I'm recorder my partner's window is down. These two guys are arguing and yelling you Niger this, you Niger that, they keep yelling, so I say, "excuse me, hey", I want to ask you guys a question, so they stop. I say," why is it, you guys call each other Niger this Niger that, and if I'd call you a Niger, and

Through the Eyes of a Cop

you get pissed off, why?" They both look, didn't say a word, "can I have your licenses and registrations, please." Inquiring minds want to know.

I was riding with my ex partner. We're driving down the block, I see this elderly white couple. The man is sweeping. I told my partner to stop, I have a feeling something is wrong. So we stop and get out. We went into his house. What happened was this. This young big black woman, around thirtyish, just took over their house, she took over, they didn't even know her, they never saw her.

We see her at the stove, she has the fire going and something in the frying pan, she has her hand on the handle and looking at us, my partner is in the rear, he says, Al," theirs oil in the pan, didn't even dawn on me. I think I backed up a bit, he might have had his hand on his weapon, she took her hand off the pan, and we walk her outside. I don't remember if we took her to the G building. Two heads are better than one. Thank you Henry. This is a strange neighborhood, there's no Mr. Rogers here.

I heard about this new program that was out It was called R.I.P. this stood for "Robbery Enforcement program". In the precinct I knew of two police officers that were In It. These two guys were the team that found the perp. that assaulted me and found out where he lived and they gave me the address. Well anyway I went Into the Inspectors office, [D.I.] and asked him if I could go on an Interview for R.I.P. He said," you know someone has to make a phone call for you", he asked me If I knew anyone; I said no, he said, he'll see what he can do. I don't know but awhile later I was called for an Interview. I'm not good at Interviews, so when I got to there. I was Interviewed by a sergeant who asked me how many collars I had, I said I didn't know, he what three hundred four hundred I said around there. Then from there another person Interviewed me, I remembered him from a precinct I worked in, he asked me, "How do you think you get Into R.I.P.".I knew the answer, but stupid me said you probably get on a list, he said ok; he gave me some paperwork to be filled out and sent me back.

Answer should have been you get in if someone makes a phone call, or you have friends in the right places.

The other Interview was with O.C.C.B. [Organized Crime Control Bureau.]When I get there, there were other cops waiting for an Interview, we sat in this room at a table one by one they were called. when they called me In I sat down In a chair and the Inspector asked me If I ever smoked pot, I said yes once I didn't like It because I choked. He asked me what would I do If someone put a gun to my head, I said something or what I would do, he said, ok well be In touch, no dice. Interviews suck. I'm good at cutting my own throat, don't need any help.

It was a Saturday, day tour. I was in the parking lot of the precinct, when a plains clothes cop approaches me. He said he was from warrants. He shows me a picture and said, they had a warrant for this guy; he was wanted for attempted murder. This guy was in a cab, and he tried to shoot the driver. Now this guy shouldn't be playing with guys, he missed.

I remember it was on a weekend. I don't know Saturday or a Sunday; I'm working with a young cop or rookie. I decided to look for him in the 71 precinct. So we circled Lincoln Terrace park, low and behold I spotted him. He was at one of the entrances' to the park. He sees the radio car. I drive slowly pass him. A little intimidation on his part he starts flexing. He was a little shorter than me, but built, and he grew a beard. I tell my partner what we might have. So I started backing up slowly, I stopped the car and we both get out. We started walking up to him casually. When there came out of the park about four young kids running up to him daddy, daddy, then they went back into the park. Remember, I'd rather talk, than start a big thing.

So when we approached him, I say, "you know you look like this guy that's wanted for attempted murder, "now listen, I know it's not you, how about we go to the precinct and clear it up, this way the other guys won't break your balls," it's like we'll give you an out of jail pass. He's was reluctant, but he agreed. I drove.

He sits in the back, no cuffs, warm day, he wearing this fitting body suit, no bulges, and weapon. My partner was in the back. We bring him into the precinct, I tell the desk officer," I have one in for investigation possible attempted murder, "he gives me a look, like what, oh Ok. We put him in the roll call room, he's sitting down, I give my partner hand signals, to keep an eye on this guy.

Well low and behold, it's the weekend, and no one works on weekends, it took me close to three hours, trying to find information on this guy. I was on the second floor with the detectives, and an Anti Crime sergeant. He looks at me and says here, me and him didn't get along; we had an incident, so I was grateful. He hands me the warrant and a picture of him.

I go down stairs, I showed the picture, to the now perp. [how titles change so fast] I say gotcha, he gives me a nod, says" yep." One under". I put in for a medal.

This might have been the second one I wrote up, I have a few. But I didn't know how to elaborate on a collar, so I never wrote them up. To make a look story short, when the paperwork came back from the Deputy Inspector, the D.I. said," I can only give it to you, not your partner, "I said, again," thanks, but no thanks; I really don't need it, "so I turned it down. It was one of two or three, I turned down. Because either my partner or another team wouldn't receive the medals. I couldn't pass the sergeants test, so what's the use. This was my last collar in the 77 precinct.

Again a bit of small information. I knew this Police Officer at the 77, real nice low speaking guy, he's on Fulton and he gets into a shootout, makes a collar, he tells me that the A.D.A. drops the charge from attempted murder to attempted assault. I was surprised. So when I made this collar, I'm taking to the A.D.A. I remembered, so I asked the A.D.A., after I told him the story, he said, is was the distance, at fifty feet it's less likely you'll hit the person, but yours since the shots fired was in a cab, less than six feet, it would be more likely you'll hit that person. Made sense, but still didn't like it, shooting at a Police Officer, should be attempted murder.

I realized I was getting anywhere at the 77 precinct, so decided to put in for a transfer. How I made my choice was, me and my wife, we're driving In Forest Hills, Queens. I didn't even know at the time that It was Forest Hills, I saw this precinct on Yellowstone Blvd. and I said this would be a nice area too work In, not even knowing that It was the Borough Headquarters, and one of the biggest mistakes In my life. You can put a suit on me, and I'll still wear sneakers.

When I got back to the 77 precinct I put a 57 In. [transfer] and the only choice I put in for was the 112 precinct. Low and behold within a month I was transferred.

FIRST TIME AT THE 112

PRECINCT

When I first got there, most of the cops were young, as of not too much time on the job. I met this young team, nice guys. I backed them up on a job, It was a dispute, and this person there was giving them orders and telling them what to do, I stood there for awhile I think they really didn't know what to do, so I stepped in took control of the situation. After the job, I explained to them, you never let anyone tell you what to do, you're always in charge. After that I make two friends

During the day tours I didn't have a steady partner, so I drove around with different guys each day. When we'd drive around, I would try to get the feel of the precinct. I spotted a bum or homeless guy walking around, which account of the area I thought was unusual. I spotted him a few more times during my tours, I said to myself that guy Is looking for trouble; I stopped him a few times just to let him know I was around and someone was keeping an eye on him. To make a long story short, sometime later, he punched a woman in the face and robbed her.

Another guy I spotted was at the opposite end of the precinct to where this other guy was. You can tell by the look and walk that he thought he owned the area; because none of the cops bothered him or went near him, so again, I made It known I was there, I used to tell him to move, he gave me a look like, he wanted to kill. Again sometime later we get a call from a store owner, again day tour, see complainant we go to this store, the lady in the store says, there's this guy playing with himself around the corner. We go outside to where he was and he's sitting in a sleeping bag and in broad daylight reading a magazine and playing with him. He doesn't even see me standing there, I hit his legs with the nightstick and told him to get the fuck out of here, he left, I could have locked him up, but I didn't. So when I used to see him, I'd stopped the car and look at him, he'd put his head down and look away. I think he was put in his place. Another Penthouse subscriber lost to Readers Digest, or wait until there's no moon out and party again, wonder if it makes you go blind, maybe that's the reason I'm wearing glasses, hmmm. Life catches up.

This other bum [ok, my day they were called Bums, today homeless people] used o walk Austin Blvd. In the winter he'd wear a short sleeves shirt and paper and plastic bags for shoes. He didn't want to get off the street so that's where he stayed. When I read that he died over the winter, account of the cold, the only thing I regretted was that I didn't buy him a pair of shoes till this day I regretted it. You can only do so much.

The other one was a homeless female. I spotted her on a four by twelve standing In a doorway of one of the stores with her bags, I got out of the car, went to her, she didn't say anything but by her body language, she cowered a little and I said hi and gave her ten dollars.

When the N.Y.P.D. joined forces with the other two police departments, Housing and Transit, we started to do some details on the train stations and platforms. I had it one night on a four by twelve. Again I saw her at the bottom of the stairs, of the train station, again with her bags, she looked at me again, I said hello, and she never talked. So I did my round for the night. I walk around a few times passed her each time; I guess without realizing it I made a routine, or had a pattern and she was making note of it.

At one point I got bored and decided to take the train, which again was not on the program. But then I remembered my shield, City of New York. So I rode the train for a few stations, came back to where I was supposed to be. This is when I saw the bag lady, she was frantic, she started telling me in body language, that I walked around and around and when I didn't show up she thought something happened to me. In other words she was looking out for me, and concerned. I was taken back, not because of that but I used to watch out for her and buy her cigarettes every once and a while, and sort of watching out for her. You never know who you're going to meet or who's going to return the favor.

I was doing an either a day tour or a four by twelve. I went down to the Queens Central Booking, on a collar I made. From the 112 precinct the D.A.'s office was moved to the courts. So for some reason and this was new to me. They didn't have an A. D.A. writing up the complaints; they had civilians, who had some title, in writing them up. So I give this guy the paper work and the information on how the arrest went down. He types it up, when I have to sign the affidavit, he says don't worry just sign it. Again those magic words, "don't worry", heard them before, that's when you have to worry, because the guy that's saying them doesn't give a fuck, and you're the one that's going to swing. So I read it, this fucking asshole decided to improvise and write what he thought it should be. I gave him a look, because talking to this shit head would have done nothing, after reading It, I crossed out, and wrote in what I did, and initialed it and gave it back. To him, he thinks it's was a game until something happens, and you're the one that signed it. Sorry for the limited vocabulary, but those words come in handy, better then jail time.

I recognized a few of the old timers there, from the Brooklyn north precincts and from the one I worked out of last. There was this tall police officer; we never spoke while we were at the 77 precinct. So when he saw me, it was either that he gave me a hi or a nod, or maybe even nothing.

I was doing a late tour and it happened that we were put together. We got a job violent family dispute. Again, I do not remember how long you have to be there. After awhile, because of the area and the precinct is a low crime area. You have a tendency of letting your guard down. I was just send there, so I was still in high gear or my senses were still sharp.

We go to the apartment. It's a high-rise building. A person opens the door, he says everything's okay, and he just wants to leave. There was no problem with the female. We both follow him back into the apartment. He goes into the bedroom, I know I'm watching him like a hawk. My partner and myself are on one side of the bed, near the doorway. He's in front of us, so he moves to the dresser and opens the drawer, he puts his hand in the drawer, before his hand comes out, I'm on him, I grabbed his hand that's in the dresser drawer, we both come up with a gun. I grabbed it out of his hand; my partner didn't even know what happened, he just stood there.

I was doing a late tour; there was a fire in one of the buildings at a specific location. I was given the fixer. I was parked on the corner facing the building, having my coffee when I heard a noise coming from the inside of the building and some yelling. I got out of the car. Went to the side entrance of the building, all the floors were gutted, burnt and shelled. I started going up the stairs slowly, figuring they could collapse. When I got to the third floor there was this person sticking out of the floor and who wasn't supposed to be there. He fell through the burnt out floor, yelling for help. I guess he might have been doing some late night shopping. I called Central, I told them what I had, and called for Emergency Service to respond. Within minutes, a couple of cars from the precinct came to see what was happening. I started to walk towards the guy, hoping maybe I could free him, this other cop, the one with the violent family dispute, the one where I came up with the gun, pulled me back, and instead, he went forward, just then from the outside of the building. I saw a ladder and another cop from an Emergency Service Unit, his head sticking up from the outside of the building, so the cop that went ahead of me, back off.

From the floor below, there were other E.S.U. Police officers. They pushed this guy's leg up and forced him to the above floor. This person was drunk. I thanked the guys, they left. I went back to the radio car, sat. I let this guy leave.

I finished my coffee. This guy comes back starts, screaming and yelling, I got out of the car and told this fucking idiot that he could have been locked up, and to take a fucking walk, me personally I think that's what he wanted to be locked up. I would not accommodate him. Hate late tours. In addition, I think this person got the shit scared out of him. No thank you, thankless job. I think the other cop was making up for dispute in the apartment.

Day tour, the sergeant gave me a job, go to one of the hospitals to guard a prisoner. I was working with a rookie. When we get there, we went to one of the hospital's rooms where the prisoner was. The room looked like a small emergency waiting room. We relieved the police officer who was there. He told us that there was a fight between this person and a doorman at one of the buildings. They both pulled out knives, he was stabbed. He killed the doorman. So we're waiting for the detectives to come down. One of the, I guess either a male nurse or an intern comes over to me, he says, the prisoner just asked him," how many cops are out there", it was a heads up. I said Thanks.

The doctor calls me into where he was behind a curtain enclosure. He asks me to give him a hand. I said ok. There was this big, what looked like a magnifying glass, this guy was cut on the arm, very deep cuts' I asked the doctor what he was doing, he said was giving him internal and external stitches. His arm looked like a filleted veal cutlet. It didn't bother me, I figured, maybe the doctor was nervous. That's ok, gave me time in the operating room. When the detectives came, I told them what the intern said, than left. I wonder if it's good to put on my resume, doctor's assistant.

I was driving one of the sergeants, from one of my past precincts. Nice person very thorough and a go-getter. He's telling me, when he was a detective in one of the Manhattan precincts. His boss tells him, that there's this guy who's doing burglaries and making a problem for him, so when you find him," I don't want to see him anymore." So they get a job, burglary in progress. They go to the location, and go to the roof of one of the buildings, they see a rope attached to the building with this guy climbing down, he looked up, and he sees them. They remembered what the boss said. So they cut the rope. They don't see him anymore. They solved the boss's problem. When I asked him a question, by the look on his face, he almost shit. I think because he was talking and getting it out and he thought I wasn't listening. Hey, listen, not my fault. De JaVu from my Midtown North Precinct, I said," no don't drop him".

I get a memo; I have to go to traffic court for a red light summons that I gave in the 77 precinct at least five years prior. I didn't realize that a person can hold a summons that long and not be found guilty, for not showing up sooner, a lot sooner. When I get there, I waited outside the room. I didn't even remember what he looked like. Nevertheless, I know I give out good reds, I mean, I didn't at the time, and my entire career on the job never gave out a yellow for a red light. The light had to be a steady red for you to get a red light summons from me.

I'm waiting, I feel like there's something fishy, because all of the cops even the ones that signed in after me were being called before I was to be called. When I was called in, there was no one else, except the complainant, the judge, and me. So we're standing in front of the judge, I go through the routine, name, rank and shield number. But I feel like this judge in hawking me, in a way I didn't like [hawking, meaning looking at me with a certain uncomfortable glare] and I mean hawking. I don't remember this guy at all, so the judge tells the complaint to tell his story. I know he's not telling the truth, just by what he's saying, I'm trying to think of what happened. All of a sudden, the complainant said something, not pertaining to the summons, but a phase, that he said, when I gave him the summons. Than bang, it brings me back to the red light, I remembered.

Now it's my turn, I start talking this judge starts hitting me with all kinds of questions, and all I mean all kinds of questions. He's really giving me the third degree, hard looks and a hard time. I figured this was a fix, I looked out at the door, there were cops standing there listening. I mean listening to what was going on. I'm there for at least twenty minutes to a half hour, very unusual. The judge is getting pissed at me, now I know it's a fix. I wouldn't give in. I had a strange feeling that the cops at the door were supporting me, because of the length of time the judge had me there. I wouldn't budge, because I knew what I was talking about. After all that time, he looks at the person, bang guilty. The judge, if looks could kill, I would have been dead. When I walk out, I got a good feeling from the cops in the doorway. After a while, more cops started to look in while I was testifying. Thanks for the support.

It was a day tour. Meet complainant, in the subway. Again, I'm working with a young cop. We go into the subway, there are four guys and a handicap girl, the complainant states these four guys raped this girl. We arrested the four. The girl had to go to the hospital. We go up to the R.M.P., now we have a first-degree rape collar. I am not at this precinct to long. So I don't know what it's about. I'm the driver, this other team, and this tall guy I didn't like from the beginning when I saw him. This was his first precinct, he though, he was Mr. Cop. He starts talking to my partner for the day, he's trying to convince him, and they wanted the collar. I'm listening, and they're acting as if I'm not even there, wouldn't be the first time. He looks at me, I said give it to them. In the 77 precinct, I had a number of rape first-degree collars. It was routine, no big thing . . .You'd have a riding D.A. show up at the precinct. Forgetting and not even thinking about what kind of a precinct this was. Here this was a big collar, and they knew.

They took the collar. The next day, Newsday paper, had on page three, a two-column spread. Two police officers, their names included, grab four guys, in the rape of a retarded girl. I told my wife at the time, see, this, I made that collar, and gave it to them, I didn't realize, it was a Political precinct and that it was big news, because of the rarity of the arrest. Sometime later, at the Whitestone pound. I saw the cop that I gave the collar to. He was wearing the gold shield. Now I know why I didn't like that other cop, now this one. Back stabbers, always took cops as my family, even family sucks and can turn against you. Still naive after all these years, or how about another beer.

I use to get Alexander's foot post plenty, during the day tours. There were a lot of foot men around from the task force, so there was company. There was this one day, when a police officer was killed, in that area. They gave me the foot post. There was no task force around. I knew and felt something was going on, because I felt alone and the only guy on the block, except for, there were a lot more Rastafarians walking around, they looked at me I looked at them. This was unusual for a white neighborhood. When I went back to the precinct, I mentioned this to the desk officer. That I thought something was happening in that area. This happened to be the desk officer, the lieutenant, that I knew didn't like me. So whatever he did and I know he did nothing. Because he was a paper man, not a street cop and again nobody likes to make waves in this precinct, because it was Queens Headquarters. We had a thing later on, not this, which I'm going to write about. I noticed some bosses who had no balls would pick on the guy doing his or her job, because it was easy and the guys screwing up or doing bad things they would pass up, or let slid. Just an observation and truth, still didn't hinder me from doing my job, because the bosses that helped over rode them.

I use to walk to my post to Alexander's, he would get pissed, this lieutenant and tell me to take the bus; I still walk to my post. He always had nothing to say. I remember three lieutenants. One, a Spanish guy, who said, Al I'd worked with you any day, another from Brooklyn north, don't remember what precinct, very intense, he's the one that I came in early one day, because I had a day tour to do and I wanted to speak to him. He was at the desk. The intense one, I went behind the desk. I said I like to speak to you. He came over, I told him," I mean do we have a problem me and you," he looked at me, he said no, I said," are you sure" he said yes, I said," because I was getting the feeling we had" he reassured me, there was none, I said," ok" and got dressed. From there, I knew he looked at me different, he's the one that told me, go look at a crime scene of a hit and run and called me P.I. Private Investigator.

Doing a day tour. I was on foot post and walked back to the precinct, as soon as I walked in to the precinct, I see the desk officer, I said, lieutenant, now this is the Spanish one, I smell smoke. He comes around from the desk. We open the door that leads to the second floor, the stairs are full of smoke, and we go to the second floor. He took a fire extinguisher with him. We open the door to the hallway. I see a door open, there's a box holding the door open, and what looked like a plastic bottle on the box, with some kind of liquid in it. He was going to go towards the room, I blocked his way. I don't know, but the first thing that I thought of, was someone set it up, the bottle might have some kind of fluid that might explode. So we went back downstairs, just in time, for the fire department to show up, they took over, and we stayed downstairs. I went to the locker room. When I came up from the locker room, that's when he said "Al, I'd work with you anytime." Made me feel okay. Nice guy, even before that, quiet man.

More tad bit of information. While at the 112 precinct, twice I did plain clothes. Both times, with these two young police officers, First one, I think it was near Metropolitan Ave and around Yellowstone Blvd., don't remember if it was for purse snatching or robberies that were going down in that area. We stood at certain locations or walked around. Nothing, I think this precinct, everyone had a chance to do plain clothes.

The second was. We hung out around 75th avenue and Austin blvd. There were commercial buildings stores and the train station. Again, we walked around, hung out. It was nice, nice guys to work with.

The guy said he had a carry permit, he showed me the carry license, first he should have told us what he was doing; second it could have ended a lot different. I took the gun opened the chamber and took the bullets out, put them in my pocket. I gave him back the revolver. We let him leave; my partner didn't say a word. When we got back into the car, he said, "you know we should voucher the bullets", we passed a corner, I told him to stop, leaned out of the car door, threw the bullets down the sewer, then we drove off. Nothing was ever said about that again. Still you have to be on your toes, but I can understand what a precinct like that could do. I hate paperwork.

112PCT

I was in a precinct where there were a lot of high-rise buildings and there were signs like Manhattan, that no matter where you went, you couldn't park and there were a lot of commercial stores in the area. So I decided not to give out any summons. When the month was over and the activity reports were to be handed in. I put down no parking summons on my report. my sergeant, nice Italian guy, from one of the Brooklyn north precincts, came over to me, and said, Al, you gave no summons out, and I told him, how the fuck are these people going to park, If there's signs all over, stating not to park. He just looked.

I did give a summons to a car, which doubled parked, In front of a parking space, the next month the same thing. He comes over, and says Al; the Inspector is breaking my balls and to do something about the summons Issue. I said, ok, if he's breaking your balls I'll give out some summons. So for that month I gave out four. I get a little note from the Inspector about the summons I gave out. He said, nice work, you're doing a great job. I guess account of my summons activity going up four hundred percent for that month. I mean who can tell, I don't know.

I was doing a day tour again, another young cop. we got a burglary in progress in one of the high-rise buildings. We went to the floor, we saw this guy, and he looked like he didn't belong in the building. We saw one of the doors tampered with. We took him back to the precinct and we're going to lock him up for attempted burglary. I told the desk officer, a lieutenant, who again, I don't think, we saw eye to eye. We were in a room where you process the prisoners. This guy keeps telling me that he was there to see a friend. He gives me a name and address. So I tell the desk officer, I wanted to check out the witness. He says lock him up, let the courts decide. I tell him, no way, I'm going to check his story. He's looking at me, he's pissed, telling me lock him up, no, I know that he's bull shitting me, so does the lieutenant. But it's that one chance that he might be telling the truth and I don't like to put someone through the hassle of the court system, for something that would take me only five minutes to check out.

So I sent a radio car to the location where I arrested him, to check out his story, it just took five minutes. I locked him up for attempted burglary. No big thing, no sweat no gain. Not going to make friends and influence people this way, but sleeping well at night.

Day tour, we took a job; accident on Queens Blvd. when we get there. There was a car up against the wall of a building. I saw a female on the ground, there was another female with her. when I knelt down beside the female on the ground the one that was injured, her leg I don't remember which leg, was completely off, except for a piece of skin holding It together. Her leg was cut off mid thigh. I took my belt off, a crowd starting to gather, including some of the police officers, who wanted to see. That's after we put a call in for the bus forth with. The person that was with the injured woman, was passing my, and happened to be an off duty nurse, and she was putting pressure on the woman's artery. She saved her life without a doubt; she would have bled to death. I told the other cops, to move the crowd back. The ambulance came and took her away to the hospital. I took down the nurse's name and address and phone number.

I spoke to the woman who was driving the car. She was like, totally distressed. Her story was, she was parked on Queens Blvd.

took her car out of park, put It in reverse. She was parked close to the corner. The gas pedal got stuck. The car whipped around the corner went up on the sidewalk, hitting this person who happened to be getting out from work and severing her leg.

We were going to the hospital for identification of the aided person. But before we went, we stayed parked at the accident scene, doing more paper work. When this guy comes up to the radio car, he says he's been waiting for his mother to arrive, and she hasn't returned from work. My partner and I look at each other. I asked what does she look like. I don't think at that time we had a name, he says, she's small, blond hair. So far, she's fitting the description of the woman taken to the hospital. We're about to tell him, about the accident, all of a sudden, his mother comes up from behind him, saying," the trains were late." a movie couldn't have done It better, thank God.

I go back to the house or the precinct. I tell my sergeant, that I want to put in a civilian commendation for the nurse, and I hate paperwork. He gives me the forms. I'm filling them out, he looks over my shoulder, and he says," Al, why don't you put yourself in." I turned, looked at him, "you know serge, I didn't even think of It." I finished the paperwork, gave it to the police officer who handles it.

I never heard anything about It. Sometime later. When they took my guns away, I went back to the precinct for some job. I saw the police officer whom I gave the paperwork to, about the civilian commendation. This guy has been at this precinct a long time, older and on the job longer, never in a high crime precinct. Thinking he was slick, and I'd forgotten about it. I asked him, whatever happened to that civilian commendation, I put in, for that nurse. He had a shocked look on his face, like stunned, figuring I wouldn't follow-up on It. he said nothing, I gotten the impression, they didn't put It In. Why, who knows, they say, it's your hair dresser, who knows for sure. Showing my age.

It was a day tour. I was driving this sergeant. I don't think he was ever in a high crime precinct either. The reason that I'm saying this about cops or bosses, not being in a high came place, Is because they act and think different, than a cop or a boss who has been there. I've been in both areas and I could relate to both types of cops. But again you can get cops and bosses who have been there and pretend to be doing the job. Go figure. So either way you have to figure it out, who to and who not to. [talk to]so we're on Queens Blvd. we picked up an accident on the main road of Queens Blvd. two cars, first car, driver, female second car driver, male. Second car hits her from behind. We're there, I checked the second car. He has his door open; I could see a roach in the ash tray, [pot]. He has one foot out of the car, he's attempting to leave. I tell him to stay here. He's Insisting, he wants to leave and tries to go through me. So I take him down, In the middle of Queens Blvd. I'm on top of him. I see a crowd gathering. The sergeant is standing over, looking at me. He's just standing. I cuffed him, take the pot, and put him In back of the radio car. Finish the paperwork. We head back to the precinct.

I locked him up, for dis-con, resisting, attempted assault, possession of a controlled substance, and driving while under the influence, and trying to leave the scene of an accident. He's sitting and I'm sitting in the process room starting the paperwork. He's trying to tell me, that he's the nephew of some politician. I couldn't care less. He makes a phone call, as I'm doing the paperwork. Sometime later, a police officer, in plain clothes comes in the processing room. I recognized him, as one of the instructors, from the outdoor range. He shows me his shield. Tells me that's his cousin. And names the politician who's his uncle. He wants me to cut him loose, can't do. He tried to leave the scene and then he put his hands on me. No good, he left.

At this time, the District Attorney's office was on the second floor of this precinct and Central Booking was on the first floor of the precinct, right beside the front desk. This was before they moved it to the court house. So I take him upstairs to the D. A.'s office.

It looked like they were waiting for me. One of the A.D.A.'s was looking at me with an expression, like; I'm not touching this guy. Now I'm figuring that a phone call was made. I don't remember if he was trying to tell me or hinting, for me to re-think what I was doing. I told him, hey I locked him up; you do whatever you want with this guy. Then I took my paperwork to Central Booking downstairs. They all knew what was going on. There was this, I remember, black sergeant. I'm saying this, because, I think our paths crossed again at the Whitestone Pound. He look at me like, I was getting a raw deal. I told him, I don't give a shit, I got names, and they can do whatever they want. I walked out. They probably voided the arrest. I think, if I had to do the job all over again, I wouldn't change a thing, I would get better and more aggressive, ah, love this job. No shit.

That black sergeant, I'm sure was the boss who came to the Whitestone Pound, he talked to me saying, you know you made history being In the Buddy Boy's book. And after that he started to become paranoid. He told me that when he was riding his bike, someone intentionally tried to run him down. After that he wanted out of the pound. Well one of the Police Officer's husband tried to run me down intentionally while I did my walk on the outside of the pound. I recognized his van. I told his wife, probably the jealous type, myself married at the time. Things happening so fast. My other book Side by Side With Heart and Mind, and a few others of my writings, are in the Library of Congress. Just blowing my horn, nobody else will do it.

I was doing day tour, when there was a cop shot in the 104 precinct. I decided to take a ride there for the search of the perp. When we get to the location of where he was shot, from there we decided to search the area. What made me get out and go to this building, who knows? Maybe a four or five story building

The first door I knock on the person that open it, I know she wasn't expecting me, because the door was opened a little too much, it was a gambling den. I told her I'm not here for that, told her what for, she seemed like she knew nothing and they were too busy playing cards, maybe four or five card tables, nice setup.

The same thing came over the air shootout in the 77 precinct. So again I decided to take a ride, this shield with the City of New York does wonders. When I get there, there were cops standing in front of the precinct, they're talking. I got out of the car, it stuck out like a sore thumb, Queens precinct on it, I was listening, some team I think it was my old partner, they had a perp in the R.M.P. he had a gun, And they said my old partner shot and killed him. No cops were injured, so I felt better and left.

On a twelve by eight tour, they had me fly to the 102 precinct for the five midnight tours. I hooked up with a young cop, who seemed like he was going to show me the ropes. This was the precinct at the time the big news was. This young girl, while going to the store was abducted and killed. He drove to where she was found. Very secluded and out of the area place, shame.

When I was in the precinct, I met a sergeant who I knew from the 77 precinct, later I would meet him again a psyche servicers, where they took mine and his guns away, but he happen to be working there.

We get a burglary in progress at the 102, he's driving I'm recorder; I spot these two guys sitting on outside stairs. At this time of night, I tell him to make a turn, we get out, talk to them a found a bag of goodies. We have two under Central. I tell him he has the collar. Another night there's a foot chase, I'm in a car, see it decide to join in, we corner this guy in an alley, they seemed very reluctant to search him, because he was grimy so I searched him, one of the other team took the collar. I went back to the 112 precinct after the fifth tour. Nice break.

On a four by twelve, I was in the house. They brought in an off duty Police Officer. He was drunk and on Queens Blvd, waving his gun. So they put him in a room, they said, "Al watch him," I knew that when you take in a cop for doing something wrong a boss has to watch the cop. So I'm standing at the door, which was open and now he insisting that he wants to leave, moving forward like chest to chest, I convinced him that he should stay, what happened after that, who knows. I went back out.

112PCT & PSYCHE SERVICES

AND SECOND TME AT THE

POUND

My downfall from the 112 precinct, It was a day tour. We received a burglary in progress at a certain location, a high-rise building and we got there first. The door was ajar, a little point of interest, we have our guns out and not only did the residents come out and interfere with us, they were actually talking and stepping In front of us. trying to be polite and tell them to go back inside, no response, they only moved when I got a little loud and direct, In other words nasty, I mean like no common sense.

As of this time there wasn't any back up, so I told my partner I'll go to the roof, just remembered it was the top floor of the building, If there was anyone In there he could flush them out through the window. So I'm on the roof of the building sitting on the edge. There was a fire escape and ladder right under me, from the apartment that was being burglarized. When I see this head and body looking out the window facing in the opposite direction of me, I yell don't move this fucking asshole turns around, now remember I have my gun on him, and says quit breaking my fucking balls. I'm a new guy in the precinct and I have no idea who he is.

Who is it? It's this ass hole lieutenant in plain clothes, yelling at me, I told him I almost shot you, he didn't give a shit. I'm new to the precinct, and according to him I should know all the guys in plain clothes, Anti Crime came to the scene, with him In charge, they never put It over the air that they were responding, no color of the day, and I'm breaking his balls. The place was empty and we left. We secured the premise. After that we talk to the super, we told him what had happened. We told him, tell the tenant what happened and if there was anything missing to call the police, they'll send a car and take a report.

After that I get a 10-02 come back to the house and see this lieutenant. so I go to his office, this fucking moron starts fucking screaming at me, and I mean screaming, this was account of the job we just had, I had no Idea of what he was talking about, so I sat on his desk my back up against the wall, my feet up and I let him yell. I waited till he was finished, than said," is there anything else"? And walked out. I'm walking down the hallway this new sergeant that was promoted and sent to the 112 precinct, I knew him by face from the 77 precinct. Young guy worked by himself didn't speak very much too any one and gave out summons. Every time I saw him with a car stop I made sure I stopped the R.M.P. waited for him to finish, made sure the car he stopped left, and then leave. We never talked. he took me behind this stairway door; stairs leading down and said remember they didn't have the color of the day on, yea, I know. Again, that's the only time he spoke to me I guess he remembered. Thanks for looking out.

This office I was in, there was an opening at the far wall, and the other side was the, either he was an Inspector or a D.I. I remember I was called into the Inspector or D.I's office he tells me, sometimes what we do here if the robberies are to high we knocked them down to grand larcenies, why he told me this who knows, new guy setting the ground work. Looked, said okay, and left.

Day tour. We get a fire in one of the gated high rise buildings. My partner stood down in the lobby of the building with some of the fire personnel. I went up to one of the floors, followed some of the fire guys and the hose. There's smoke in this hallway, I'm walking around, and I see an elderly woman in a house dress walking around. I tell her to follow me, she say this ways better, so I followed her. We end up back in the lobby, she says she's OK. My partner is still talking in the lobby; we go back to the precinct. We notify the desk officer, I say I'm a little dizzy, he says go to the hospital to make sure you're OK. My partner drove me to the hospital. The doctor checked me out, they might have given me a little oxygen, he said smoke inhalation, and I put on my shirt went back to the precinct, again told the desk officer. Don't remember if I went home sick.

A day tour we had an aided case. We get there, there's this huge guy in bed, breathing difficulty, I get on the bed and try to arrange the pillows, the ambulance attendants arrive and they're going to take him to the hospital. So all four of us are heaving and hoeing. Finally we get him in the bus. I'm working with a young cop. They transport, we followed get to the hospital, and do an aided card, notifications and back on patrol. We get a 10-02 back to the house, they say that the guy that we transported to the hospital, has hepatitis, so we go back to the hospital, my partner, he starts making phone calls to his mother, he's very nervous. The sergeant comes into the hospital, he says what's going on, why didn't you stop him from making calls to his home, hey serge, how am I supposed to know, his father was a captain on the job, his mother probably called the precinct, hey go figure.

It was day tour, and I was told I'd be a driver for an Inspector, we were to go to the 102 precinct, I think the location was Jamaica Queens, a precinct with a bit more crime. When we get there, he gets out of the car and he stands in the middle of an avenue looking around. I think at the time there was a problem there with the community. So he's standing there looking around. Not too many people or traffic around, he tells me, see that social club, get them off the sidewalk and off street. I go there and tell them my boss wants you off the sidewalk and inside, they're all looking at me not moving. Then I say if you don't, I start locking people up, which a collar is a collar anywhere. Now I guess the take me seriously. I remember some were standing and some were sitting on chairs. The guys sitting on the chairs got up first and started to move in, the others followed.

On the way back to the precinct we stopped on Austin Blvd. right near the subway entrance and he wants to clear the cars from the bus stop that were parked there, so he does. He starts yelling in the car," anyone likes this job needs a psychiatrist", I turned faced him; I tell him "I love this job". A short time later I'm at the T.S. or phone operator. I hear the lieutenant at the desk say, "no Inspector Cimino's not around". And he hangs up. I didn't say anything, I made it pass.

I get called into the lieutenant's office. This time it's another lieutenant, an Italian guy. he tells me they would like me to go to psyche services, I said is this, a request, he says." Yes", I say." No', then he says," don't make me order you", I thought it was a request; I was just testing the waters. So I made or they made the appointment. Nice, anyone who likes this job. Hmmm.

The day of the appointment, it's In Queens. I go up to the floor and see a sergeant who I recognized and knew from the 77 precinct, he was working there, the same guy from the 102 precinct. We greeted each other. He tells me like; he flipped out and is working here. He now is going to make me meet the Inspector that's in charge he says," he's here, he's a fucking nut, they took his guns," something to do, he wanted to shoot his wife. We go into the office, he sees me, and says," don't tell me another fucking nut job," I started to smile, shaking my head. We left the office, we played catch up. We talked in a room, and at this point I didn't trust anyone. So I just listened.

I stayed there for the day; I guess they were deciding what to do with me. By mid afternoon I was taken back to the precinct In an unmarked car with a plain clothes police officer, they were going to take my guns away, they labeled me a burn-out, physically, emotionally, and mentally a burned out.

So we went to the precinct I went to the locker room on my own, I guess they thought I wasn't a suicide case, took out my gun, went back up stairs told the driver my off duty was at home. So he drove me to Little Neck in Queens, we went to my house. I went in, got my off duty and handed it to him, both weapons were vouchered at the precinct and I was handed a copy of the receipt. I stayed there for a week or so until they decided what to do with me. Then I was told I was going to be transferred to the Whitestone Pound until I got my guns back. I was told indirectly that I would have my weapons back within nine months.

ON LIMITED DUTY AT
WHITESTONE POUND

The first lieutenant, I met there I knew him as a sergeant In the 77 precinct we talked a while said that he has worked at most of the precincts In the city, because he used to get bored staying at one place to long, and every time he moved around a scandal broke out at the precinct that he was in. He'd stayed for a while then left. Welcome to another three ring circus.

Meeting this other boss at the pound was an experience. I found out he was a lieutenant from I.A.D., Internal Affairs Division. I remember standing in the middle of the floor. The buildings were like Mobil trailers one floor. He's talking to me and one of his sergeants was looking like he was going to kick the shit out of me. I felt like he was coming after me, so I went after him, the lieutenant called him off. They sent me to what was called the tower. It was a room about two stories off the ground, about six by six feet with a stool and a small table coming out of the wall. You were supposed to be a look-out for anyone stealing, or helping someone find his or her car or truck. You could see most of the yard on your side. In the yard there were two towers, one on each side of the pound, you also had a pair of binoculars.

When I first got to the Whitestone Pound these were the first guys that I met. Most were there, as transfers from other precincts and considered old timers. These guys ran the pound, like this old gang of mine. As usual when a new police officer comes to any precinct or detail it's hard to get in, because if something is going on they want to make sure you're not a plant from F.I.A.U. [Field Internal Affairs Unit.] or I.A.D. [Internal Affairs Division,] and since the 77 precinct was in the process of lock-ups or suspensions and who were the rats, and they, which is the Department, getting started with the arrest cases and so on. And I happen to work at the 77 at the time, when everything was going on and I transferred out just before the finally. They were on guard, so as usual I sat and observed and got to know the players.

In the In-take room, your job was to take in the vehicles, that were to be vouchered, check the paperwork to make sure it was done correct, search the vehicles for drugs and weapons or anything of value that should have and supposed to have been vouchered at the precinct. If there was anything found the accompanying officer takes it and has to voucher it by calling there precinct and getting a voucher number for that item or items. One cop. a young guy that worked with us in intake, he was like a blood hound, he found a few weapon and drugs.

As for me, I found one handgun as I searched this auto. It was on the driver's side of the car, at arm's reach, under the dashboard. As soon as he or whoever was driving, just had to bend a little, reach and the gun was right there and in your face. I gave it to the cops who brought in the car and they had to voucher it. You'd get a little pissed because the cops who stopped the car could have been killed or seriously wounded for not searching the car and if we didn't find the weapons, when they came back for the car they got the car and there gun back.

One of the guys who worked in In-take and was waiting to retire, he worked at another job in a huge fitness center. I think he ran it and on the side he did carpentry. He said that he was building a house somewhere upstate, nice guy. After he got to know you, he became a little friendlier. Another guy, me personally, I think at one time he ran with a Bikers club, that's the impression he was given me, and from what the Lieutenant told us.

This Lieutenant, was former I.A.D., went to Florida. So this cop gives him and address of a bar to visit, the bar turns out to be a biker's bar. The Lieutenant comes into the intake room, says, "What were you trying to get me killed; they were all bikers in that place "good laugh. And yes maybe he was. I doubt it.

Another guy they called him the Reverend, he carried the bible around and preached and believed in Jesus. He was preparing for retirement. He bought one acre of farm land from an Amish farmer, which they rarely sold to anyone besides their own, and he was building a house in that area. He was a Manhattan police officer, nice guy. When he retired he gave some people a map and directions to his new home, myself too, I wanted to call and visit. I never did and now that I'm in Pennsylvania too, maybe one day I'll look him up and give him a call.

Another police officer tall, quiet, very low keyed, I saw him once, when they accused him of something, he was ready to go at it with the bosses. I and another cop stood up for him, he always played the lottery. Sometime after I retired, I heard that he hit for three million dollars, that's what was going around, whether true or not, it couldn't have went to a better person. He said he was a sergeant in the Arm Forces.

These first guys I met, were there quite some time and were either waiting to retire or just buying their time or hanging on to this detail. That's when I went to the pound for the first time.

When I was put on limited duty and they took my guns away. This group not all but most was like a gang that was there a long time and they ran the place, not the bosses. I felt like again, they were very cautious of me because I had worked in the 77 precinct and because of the 77 scandal just coming into view and they might have thought I was a turn coat and wired, again all speculation. I felt like some of them were trying to intimidate me directly or indirectly threatening me. So I had to feel it out and see.

One guy and Italian guy wanted to show me how crazy he was. I was with him, we were in the back of the pound, riding on one of the machines, and this one had a bucket. So he decided that he was going to knock down one of the utility poles, so he starts slamming this machine into it and trying to take it down, I figured if he does, I was ready to jump out, because this machine was starting to tip over. After a few tries he looked at me and stopped. Me personally at the time I really didn't give a fuck, if he took it down or not, he made no impression on me, except that he was an idiot. After that, once or twice he came after me. We were in the release trailer, he came after me, I just stood my ground, this one tall guy, grabbed him and was holding him back. I just looked at him.

There was this motor cycle cage, where they stored all the motor cycles that were taken in for safe keeping, evidence, or had been in accidents and the ones that were not going to be returned were auctioned off. The police officer, old timer that took care of the cage, wasn't too friendly, when he looked at me I always felt like there was something going on other than police work.

Well there was this stayed dog that came into the pound that he started to take care of it. One day he had him tied up to the entrance of the cage, the dog was barking, I saw his tail wagging so I got close to it and he bit my leg. When I went Into the pound, I told the boss, the cop that took care of the bikes was there too, he just looked at me and said," why didn't you kill It", I said," for what, the dog was tied up, so why should I kill it". This guy was taking care of this dog made him an attack dog without telling me. So when a dog's tail is wagging, doesn't mean there happy to see you. After that they made him get rid of the dog. I never hit a cuffed prisoner, so why shoot a tired up dog?

The first time that I was indirectly threatened is when I found my tire cut, I was pissed, I came back to the trailer fuming, told the lieutenant, he said some bull shit words to make me relax and I made out a UF 61 report. I'm pretty sure I found out who did It. During the day I used to like to walk around the pound, get a little exercise, just sitting wasn't my thing. So one day I see this police officer, who was there a while, this guy when he retired moved upstate with his In-laws, I see him, he had this big screw driver and he puts it through one of the tires of a cars that was parked on the lot. He saw me, then he leaves, I went to the car I looked at the tire, It was the same type of hole that was given to me outside the pound, I figured it was him that did my car, and he was told to do It. He never talked just used to look at me, you know the strong silent type, and he wore glasses. If the shoe fits wear it, or was that Cinderella?

The second time that my car was damaged. I just bought a new Buick Grand Sport. That day I went on a detail and came back late that night. When I drove my car I felt something was wrong. So I took it to the Buick dealer, the mechanic came back to me and said two or three of your lugs have been snapped off, he said it looks like someone did it. They replaced the thread and nuts. I came back to the pound made out a report, I went into the In-take room, and I spoke to one of the brothers who worked there, there were three brothers who worked at the pound. I spoke to the older one, he did time in the street, high crime, I said, hey [name] I told him what the mechanic said, he looked at me and I saw on his face concern, he said, I think someone is trying to kill you, OK. Needed this like I needed an income tax audit. Now, being very careful. When I received the death threat from a call from the T.S. operator, that was from a drug dealer, and the lieutenant on the desk, said," you'll be getting plenty more", didn't realize some would come from the inside. Silly me.

Between all of this I was feeling a little down or angry, because leaving the 77 precinct not getting anywhere with the job and being put on limited duty. So I decided to put this negative energy into use. I decided to take up Martial Arts, where I left off, before coming onto the job. I left one place as a green belt in the style of Go Ju. So I picked up where I left off and took a style in Kempo Karate.

I was in the In-take room for some time these guys that were in there with me were seasoned veterans who have been on the street, and just trying to keep out of trouble and get off the job. There was one guy there who was there because of a drinking problem and trying to get out on three quarters. Tall thin guy with glasses. I don't think we saw eye to eye. He use to take care of the cars and steal little things out of them. I think it might have annoyed some of the police officers, but he thought he was slick. It got to me, so

I told him one morning hey [his name] I didn't realize the stores were open this early for shopping, he gave me a look; he had no guns just like me. We met in the, what they called the lunch room, It was a filthy dirty trailer; I thought we were going to go at it, but he just left. They vested him out of the job.

I met him one summer at Long Beach in Long Island, where I used to walk on the broad walk. He was at this food place, I saw him on the broad walk, he spotted me, and so I walked up to him said hello. We talked a little then I moved on. He was telling me that he was looking at and what sounded like, he had a crew and they were looking to steal Porsches. He looked like one of these guys, if you didn't know him, you'd hand him a buck. I was wondering if he was talking to get some kind of a response or reaction from me, or he was stealing cars. Sometimes you do and sometimes you don't, it's all according to the conversation and who's talking.

They wanted me to learn the release window; I'm not sure if that was the right name. That's where the civilians and the released perps from jail would pick up their cars or trucks or motorcycles. At that time I really didn't want to be bothered with the public. I told the bosses after ten I can't count any higher, because you're dealing with money, so they never put me there. These two locations were in one trailer, plus there were two offices, and the civilians that worked there, in one big room, it was a mobile home trailer.

Once a week everyone that was there for some kind of medical or self abuse kind of thing, was sent to psyche services to speak to a physiologist, from the police department. Even before going to psyche services, I was told I'd have my guns back in nine months. So when it was my turn to go. I'd drive to this building in Queens, go to the psyche service floor, wait, and there I would meet my counselor, a very pleasant and nice person. In the beginning I was very reluctant to talk to her, but as the weeks passed I opened up. I thought they wanted me to talk about the job, because that's when the 77 precinct broke with the scandal and lock-ups and I think they wanted me to go in that direction. So when I opened up I bored her to death with my life, my marriage my In-laws, me being a new father so on and so forth. She listened, asked questions, and we sometimes talked casually about life. We hit the job a few time. I sure one day she mentioned, "Al you know, that with the job, the majority rules and you have to follow", So I said to her, "you're telling me that if there are ten guys and eight are stealing I'm supposed to steal", I got no answer.

I remember going there one day, to psyche services, and as we were talking, she came out with a statement and the statement that she came out with, I only spoke and said this to one specific guy and I used a word that she came out with, So either, everything I was saying, was going back to the bosses or this police officer who I spoke to was possible was undercover from I.A.D. or F.I.A.U. so it made me think a little more clearly about this particular guy. Before I went to the pound, I went to One Police Plaza, I went to this office, I think in the basement and was Introduced to a Lieutenant from the Field Service Bureau, that's what our branch of the service was affiliated with, the pound and I'm sure he told me he was F.I.A.U. for that area. The area would be F.S.B. or Field Service Bureau.

I was not used to being at a desk all day; many times I would walk out and walk around the pound, which was for my daily routine of exercising, because in the last two precincts they had weight rooms. When I needed more than just walking around the pound, I took my routine outside, and started to walk around the neighborhood. Another guy started to do the same thing. Before he retired, he learned how to give polygraphs and got a job with some firm doing that. One by one the old timers started to retire and new faces were coming in.

There's these two guys who work at the pound and work together, there job was to get the cars ready that were marked and going to auction. One of the guys, tall thin guy, he was the one that told me about the check that you get at the end of the year, called the supplement check. How he mentioned it was. When I got to the pound I was talking about leaving the job after fifteen years and can't wait to get out, I remember we were sitting in the trailer, where cars, after the public retrieved them from the lots, either they towed out or if they were drivable drove out. This separate trailer is where they are signed out. So he says you're not going to wait for the supplement check. I had no Idea what he was talking about. I found out later my father-in-law at the time knew about the supplement check and never mentioned it to me, and I told him I was going to get out In fifteen years. That's how much he was looking out for me, and so called wanted me in the family. So I asked what's the supplement check, and he told me, after that I knew I was going to say the full twenty. Best piece of information I've ever received on the job.

Well anyway. One day he and another cop was checking the cars, popping the trucks of the cars that were ready for auction, making sure nothing of value or any contraband was over looked by the inspections. On this day to their surprise they finds these two huge packages wrapped in bubble plastic wrap, it was two bodies, and they looked like they were neatly wrapped, broken in half and placed in the trunk of the car. How they ever made it through the precinct, then to the yard parked and stored and no one spotted it is beyond me. I'm pretty sure that was a rude awakening for him and his partner.

We used to auction off parts from motor cycles, cars, trucks and whatever the police department could make money on. I remember one rumor that was going around. that the police department O.C.C.B.[or Organize Crime Control Bureau] made a raid on the Don's brother—in—law's place and confiscated a lot of different parts from all kinds of auto's that were stolen, chop shop. They were vouchered and sent to the pound. By mistake [again you never know] they were put up for auction and sold. The parts were supposed to be the evidence for some case, for the department, against the perp. What ever happened after that, I don't know. If that really happened could have been a mistake or someone was working for them on the inside. After awhile you never know who's working for whom, and it wouldn't be the first time.

And I'll repeat what that old timer said from the 77 precinct, Al remember, everything stays the same, only the faces change. That was one of maybe four things or verbal sayings that old timers told me that helped a lot. Al just do your job you make the arrests and let the court do the rest you can't help everybody so pick the ones that have to be helped something to that effect. These things that were said helped make the job easier, and at the end of the tour you signed out and you made it home.

When the 77 precinct broke out there were I think thirteen police officers that were suspended and I was at the pound at the time. I started seeing some of the police officers who used to work at the 77. When that broke almost the whole precinct was transferred to one place or another. I started seeing old faces coming here. Some looked at me shook hands others just looked. one guy who did the steady Washington Avenue post with a younger cop came down we spoke and the only thing he said was Al, I just want to collect my pension, like I had something to do with him not collecting a pension. [This was the F.T.O. from the 77, he was standing near the gas pump, when the black F.T.O. who was standing in front of me hand on his gun, looked like he was ready to draw, I just stood there, he freak, and he started yelling it's him not me you want, it's him. I couldn't see if the other cop had his hand on his weapon. Just like the scene in the precinct, when the D.I. backed me up you had to be there to understand, then two and two does make four.] As I was listening I'm looking around and I saw we were in front of the trailer just in front of the office of the lieutenant and his window was open.

Don't know if he said it there as a coincidence or he made that statement for him to hear as if I had something to do with the lockups. after a while you never know what's going through their mind or yours, you start looking over your shoulder good guy or bad guy, doesn't matter, part of the job after awhile, whether you're good guy or bad guy, you start to get a little paranoid, sometimes that's a good thing.

Next is when this suspended police officer, he was the cop I worked with, I was driving down Eastern Parkway, and we saw this woman holding her child, she looked frantic, we stopped, she said her baby stopped breathing, the mother got into the back seat, he took the baby, I drove, and he said he gave mouth to mouth resuscitation and revived the infant. so he came down with the sergeant who was in charge of the twelve by eight crew known as [name] Raiders, they came down in a tow truck, I heard he had his own tow company. He, the sergeant, I'm pretty sure he retired before the scandal broke with the 77, so I guessed the ex cop was working for him.

One day I was standing near to the front gate, talking with one of the police officers who worked there. And he comes in again. The thing that got me, is I'm at the pound for a certain amount of months, and you don't see any of these guys from the 77 precinct, now when the shit hits the fan, they start coming in one by one, day by day, and I can't figure it out. Some are looking at me, say nothing; others are just looking, shaking my hand, giving me the eye. So now I'm wondering if they think I have anything to do with what happened there. I guess again, I'm getting a little suspicious about, first when this retired sergeant came down with the ex police officer driver of a tow truck.

They go into the auction area, the ex police officer opens one of the car doors, makes like he taking cover behind the door, as if he has a gun the retired sergeant is behind the rear of the auto. I'm standing in the open. This other sergeant who was on limited duty from Street Crime, he comes running out and sees what's happening. He starts running towards these two guys as, what seemed like a buffer, between them and me. So I figured maybe he's watching out for me, because we used to talk about what happened and why he was there. So again could be my mind playing tricks or he might have been watching out for me, or they wanted to make me break from the position I was in, because they might have thought I knew something about what happened at the precinct, being one of the partners of one of the Buddy Boys, and how could he not be dirty. Hey, you never know, or I needed a

160

drink. Sometimes good to be a little paranoid, mind does wonders with seeing a situation more than one way. When things happen to you that others don't hear or see, everything makes sense to you, others you don't really care what they think; because it's your ass on the line, like hey don't worry about it, just sign.

So again when I was at the gate this retired sergeant comes down, now you got to remember he never came down before this, he's just looking at me. so I said to myself," fuck the job, fuck the pension," If this guy Is going to do me, let's do It. so I leave this cop I'm talking to, and say, If he's going to shoot me, I might as well be ready to shoot him.I see him in his, I don't remember if he had a car or truck, he's sitting there. So I get into my car, put my gun between my legs, and pull out, I look in my rearview mirror, and see him pull out, so I drive a-little ways, pull into the curb, roll down my window, I'm thinking, if he stops and pulls along side, my gun is in hand, at least I'm read. But he passes me, so I pull out and started following him. When he gets onto the highway I stay on the road, I'm not going to follow him to his turf. I go back to the pound. That was the last time I ever saw him. He never came back to the pound. I know better safe than sorry. No one to talk to, no one to trust. And a crazy lieutenant on my heels.

Being on the job for a number of years, you really don't know who to trust. Just with the few incidents I had. the one In the 77 precinct, where me and my ex partner from the 61 precinct who came there under a cloud, that they had him and another cop on film for burglary. the guy that we locked up was going to give us names of cops who were visiting prostitutes and taking money, that was during a mid night tour and the only boss you could tell was this sergeant who retired and was in charge of the buddy boy raiders. Caught between a rock and a hard place, so you don't know who is the worst of the two evils, my ex, the boss, like who's who. That's why I took it in my own hands, to protect myself and you don't know how far up it can go, and that's with any job your own. If there's something going on that's not right. Had the same problem in Penn. With another job. Same shit different faces lost that job.

During the time on limited duty, rather than using the negative energy that I had, I decided to take up Martial Arts. I use to take it up just before I became a police officer. I took Go-Ju at the time and received my green belt. So this time I went to a Dojo that I used to pass on the way home from work, called American Olympic Karate Studio.

So I went in, my ex came with me, at the time, because she thought it was a good Idea. We went into the office spoke to one of the owners. he talked, told me what it was about, I listened and said ok. I also told him I don't want you to give me my belt, I wanted to earn it. So they gave and put with me I believe there toughest and best instructors and I mean what a work out. After a while, I myself became an instructor. It usually takes around five years or more to become a black belt. I became a black belt first degree in a little more than two and a half years. I use to practice no less than three hours a day and a lot of time five to six hours a day. And I'd say, I earned the belt and title of Sensei.

A Sensei or a black belt Instructor can only spar at this place if someone came up to me and said I would like to spar tonight, and no matter who it was, I had to spar with or kick box for another term. I had the feeling that the owner, nice guy told everyone if you beat him you get your black belt. So I had guys from all classes wanting to spar or kick my butt. No one got there black belt from me. Or maybe just to kick the shit out of some cop, it was more incentive to win on my part.

When the sergeant came around to update my profile for the police department, If you accomplished anything like going to college or any other degree, I told him I made my black belt 1st degree and It was noted on my Police record, or file.

At the pound there are these towers, two, and one on each side of the pound. Maybe standing about two stories high. You'd climb up maybe ten to fifteen stairs, up Into a trap floor door, enter, it was maybe six foot by six foot box, or room, windows all round, one shelf with a stool. From there you could see most of the pound and its activities. There was a pair of binoculars. In case anyone was stealing, or damaging the vehicles, you can spot them, or try to spot them and make an arrest, or if the office was looking for a particular vehicle or van's, and the location wasn't marked on the paperwork, they would call you, tell you what they were looking for and you would help and try to find it.

While I was up there I would practice my Martial Arts or read and again watch the activity. I spotted these two guys in suits walking down the road. They stopped in my isle where the tower was, I guess or I know they didn't see the tower, because they couldn't be that stupid. one of the guys pick-up a tire iron or he brought one with him, he probably needed a tire, so there was one on the back of a van, he starts wacking the lock, trying to break the lock and take the tire. I'm looking at this, the other guy was probably the look out, never looking up, so I go down, show them my shield, no guns, and you're under arrest. I take them both to the office; tell them what I have, the sergeant and lieutenant let them go. Like what the fuck. So what am I doing up their?

On the day of one of the car auctions, the civilians are allowed to roam around and inspect the cars. I'm in the Intake room doing the cars, I hear a little commotion. So I go out and check, they have this teenager in the sergeant's office. I heard he was checking out one of the cars, and there must have been a cassette tape in the car, so he takes it. If we would have seen the tape, we would have thrown it away. So they're going to lock him up. I put my head in the office and tell them," yea my two guys with the suits stealing and damaging the van you let go, this kid with a two dollar tape you arrest, what bull shit", I walked away, don't know what they did.

I think one day the lieutenant was with his favorite dog, his sergeant. He tells me, you know we can take you out of here in a straight jacket and have you committed, I stood there, looked at them and walked away. Funny, one fucking psycho to another. Look who's calling the kettle black. When I got my guns back, this lieutenant asked me if I wanted to come back to the pound permanently, between this and the 112 precinct, I took the better of the two evils, I said yes. For some reason, this lieutenant was a hard nose guy, but I did like him. Who knows life?

THE WHITESTONE POUND
WHEN I WAS PUT THERE
PERMANENT

In the main building there was an intake room where the police officer from N.Y.P.D. and Sanitation Police would bring in confiscated trucks, cars and motor cycles. Intake would process them there. The cops in there were either transferred there, light duty, drinkers, police who killed a person while off duty, police officer who shot there friend because he pointed a weapon at him and though it was empty and killed him, police officer who exposed themselves to a person, bribery, burglary, guys like me burn-outs, only one, or police officers who were there because of stress and couldn't handle the street, and of course the police officers who wanted to be there. Police officers who were never on the street, this was called a detail. Some days it was like a three ringed circus, nice bunch of guys, just a bunch of misfits, including myself. Or cops that turned bad, and of course our leader, the lieutenant.

On the other side, or the other end of this trailer, was where the cars, trucks, motorcycles were being picked up by their owners, or the perps that were locked up and release to pick up their vehicles or motorcycles that were in for safekeeping. I didn't want at this time with getting involved with the public so when they asked me to do that job I told them I couldn't count, again. So they put me in the Intake room. There I met some real nice guys; bad guys, crazy guys, and whatever other names you could come up with.

For a description of some of the personnel that worked there. There were a few guys there that were just waiting for retirement, real nice guys. Two guys were drunks, there were probably a lot more but two were there for that reason. One young kid, tall, blond hair real good looking guy didn't have a clue of his character, nice guy well mannered. The other, another nice guy with time on the job a practical joker. Who I can say didn't give a fuck or trust anyone. I don't remember if it was him or the other guy, who was going out with some girl who was driving them crazy, and they would go back for more punishment.

I listened to the stories about her and it was time for him to move on, but I guess when you're in love you don't see clearly, she was always jamming him up. The practical joker for instance, I would do my paperwork, go out check the car, he work reorganize or mess up the order of my papers and when I got back, he'd pretend, to be working and it's not me, look on his face., I work sit down reorganize the papers and say nothing, I go out he do it again, I'd come in reorganize them again say nothing. This went on for about half the day, until he couldn't take it any longer and blurted out, wow you don't say a thing, or he was always laughing. Nice friendly guy. He said his father was a lieutenant on the job, I think retired

I worked in the intake room long enough to learn some of their personalities. He comes in one day, the joker. I think it was a Monday, he would have these mood swings, and say, "Fuck It, I'm not working anymore," I'm pretty sure account of the time I had on the job I was like In charge or something. I knew he was a worker, so I said nothing. Day one eight hours no work, he sat there for eight hours doing nothing, second day, again, no work. I could see he was like steaming, and waiting for me to say something, third day, forth day I could tell he was going crazy, I mean eight hours of sitting and doing nothing for a guy that loved and had to work. Friday, he came walked in went to the in box and started to work, I knew if I told him "hey [J.J.] when the fuck are you going to work," his response would be "fuck you" but he was a worker and doing nothing was driving him nuts. This guy didn't give a fuck who you were he broke your balls, except the bosses.

No matter who, calling the cop who exposed himself a dickey waver, other guys, he'd say you killer so on and so forth and start laughing, me I liked him and I'm sure the feelings were mutual.

There was this Spanish guy, nice guy. My wife said to me once, "every ones a nice guy to you", while I was talking about a rapist. He had a lot of stress and into God, he lived in the Bronx. Young man, young wife, I think he said, if he wasn't pulling my leg, he had four kids. He used to break my balls, yea small apartment, my kids slept in draws, which could have meant they slept in draws or they slept in draws. He was there for a collar and they said he planted a guy on the guy he locked up. At that time he was working with a younger cop and they were putting him through hell.

He would talk and look me in the eye and tell me his story. As time went on he was out for a while. When he came back he said that he was under so much stress that he threatened to kill his whole family. That's when I told him," you know I have a house upstate and if you and your family need a break or a small vacation just to get away you can use it". I think that might have helped, knowing he might have had a friend, never took me up on it, but he knew it was there.

I also told the P.B.A. delegate, another young cop, who was there. This guy was the Fire Chief in Franklin Square, that if he wanted it, he could use the house too. He did everybody favors, he was also a mechanic who helped out the cops that worked there with their cars, he helped me and didn't charge a lot of money. He taught me how to drive some of the big rigs there, the ones that could lift the cars. Last thing I heard he got three quarters and retired.

Another Spanish guy was there for firing his gun outside; I don't know if he wounded someone accidentally. I think he was going to lose the job and was setting himself up to be a tow truck driver making some connections while there, because of all the tow companies that came and them bringing damaged cars, truck and motorcycles.

Another Spanish guy very quiet, wouldn't talk much, I guess the less said the better in the position he was in. He and some of his friends were in his or one of his friends house hanging out. He thought his gun was empty pointed at one of his friends and killed him. I got to talking to him not much but we shared some of our music together, I think he lost the job. Better than being locked up.

OUT ON THE STREET AGAIN

OPERATION TAKE BACK AND POUND

I was at the Whitestone Pound when the city declared operation take back. This was a Program implemented by the city, probably the Mayor and Commissioner of the police department that the drug dealers had taken over the city in such neighbors where drugs were running rampart, so they put the cops who were on details and precinct cops for more foot post in certain areas, to take back the streets and start making narcotics arrests.

So with about nineteen or better years on the job, they decided to put, or the lieutenant decided to put me back on the street. Just love this guy, as my ex loved me.

My first precinct was the 71 precinct in the Crown Heights area of Brooklyn, it was the bordering precinct of the 77 precinct, Eastern Parkway was the borderline for these two precincts, so I was familiar with the area, mostly, blacks and Hassidic Jews, nice combo. The Hassidic were there first and as the area started to get run down the blacks moved in.

I got to the precinct, I went to the Muster room, heard the speeches from the bosses, and soon. I saw, and started to meet guys that I knew from the 77 precinct. We just acknowledged by a look or a nod. The first run in with crime in that area, I think it was Thanksgiving Eve and I did not want to make a collar because my wife at that time makes a great dinner and we were having company. So they give me a post that bordered the 70 precinct, that's where I had a cousin working.

So I'm walking to this post and I see maybe four or five Jamaicans standing in the street blocking pedestrian traffic or impeding vehicular traffic, another name for move or you get a summons, or worse arrested.

So as I see them I stop and tell them you guys have to move you're in the way. I tell them if I come back and your still here someone is getting locked up. One guy starts laughing and pointing. I said to myself okay no problem, so I walked away.

I head for the near end of the post, where there was a train station, so I go into the station and meet some guy in uniform with no weapon. I asked him, I mean, who are you and what are you doing? He said the city hired them, I really don't know what they were called, like security guards, to watch the train stations. I felt like I've been out of the street to long, and had no clue about this. We talked a little; I went outside, stood in front of the station. That's when my cousin rode up, I haven't seen him in awhile, what are you doing here? You know that operation take back, they put me back on the street, we talked a little and he went. He was a police officer from the 70 precinct.

I walked some more. I see these guys that I told to move from before, there were only about four or five guys the first time, now there are about ten to fifteen guys. Loud music, the whole nine yards. I went back; I told them to move again, I mean nothing, no fucking response. I moved about, maybe twenty feet from the crowd. I called Central, "Central this is patrol post number so and so, can you have one car, no make that two cars. Respond to such and such location." She comes back and says," officer, what's the condition there," I come back, and say," I got about fifteen guys breaking my fucking balls," within minutes, two precincts responded.

The sergeant responded also, and numerous cars I looked at the sergeant. I thought I heard, take them, so I drop one guy and the other guy I wanted, starting to move in a way I didn't like, and I thought was threatening, so I punched him in the face, and tell both of them your under arrest. You're right, if you're thinking, the one guy was the loud mouth the other his friend. Central make that two under. Wonder if I should have done that the other way round, you're under, and then punched him in the face. Oh well still learning.

So we're in front of the desk and there's this female sergeant, the guy who was resisting arrest, the one I punched in the face. He's crying and telling her he's afraid of me and see what he did. I mean he was scared shit, but me, once you're in cuffs you're under and it's over unless you start at the precinct. So she's looking at me, now remember, I'm there, at their precinct, as a guest, and if I was reading her right, she thinking should I make a complaint for police brutality or what, so I take him to the holding cells with the other perp. I put him in the cell. He's cowering in the corner, like I'm going to kill him, so he must have been around or just playing it up. He's crying don't make him come near me; don't make him come near me, again the whole nine yards.

I give his friend a summons for impeding pedestrian traffic, I tell you these summons come in handy. The pen is mightier than the sword, ah; sometimes body language comes in handy too. The other guy is going to get a D.A.T. [Desk Appearance Ticket]. Who comes in? But the female sergeant, she's still looking at me, I didn't say a word. This guy in the cell, playing, in fear of his life. I don't remember if she talked to him, but she started to help me with the paperwork. What I figured I think she didn't know since she was a new boss if she had to make out some type of form on this prisoners complaint for being hit, but she did nothing and I think he went through the system. Because of resisting arrest.

There was this other police officer from the pound that I met there. He was in Highway until he was transferred to the pound, told a lot of good stories, whether true or not, they were good listening to, broke up the day. I didn't see him much. In this precinct I had a few run ins with the bosses. I use to see these two cops who work there. I had more time I the job but I had the feeling they didn't like me.

I came in one day and I had on a short sleeves shirt. So when I walked into the precinct, again one of the young sergeants, this time a male, comes up to me and said," do you know it didn't come up over the Tele-type that you're supposed to wear short sleeves shirts," I came back and I said." you know what? "Here's what I do, I put my head outside, and I feel for the weather, if it tells me it's warm I put on a short sleeve shirt." I guess he didn't like that answer. So from there when they gave me a foot posts. It might have been every half hour I would get a scratch, in other words, they were breaking my balls and looking to give me a complaint. I guess the cops knew, and some of the guys I used to work with, and most of the other police officers at the 71 precinct didn't know, that I use to work with some of the 71 guys.

So I remembered one of the cops that worked out of the 77 precinct, when I was working there, and I remembered him, again just the nod, or the eye contact, just to let each other know that we remembered each other. We started talking and he tells me indirectly, hey, I'm here and there picking on me, because I'm black, and he's really looking at me, hey Al again, there picking on me because I'm black and he was black, I got the message.

I'm in the Muster room, there was full house, so I stand up and start talking loud, you know there breaking my balls because I'm Italian and I believe in God, that why there breaking my balls. You want to see a room empty out. The few that stayed gave me like the high five of acknowledgement. It stopped.

Another time I get a message that the Inspector of the precinct wanted to see me. So I go into his office. I'm standing in front of his desk, young guy in a suit. He says I got a complaint that you pushed two police officers. I tell him "if I pushed someone that means I was pushed first." And I leave. The next day I'm called in again. This time he tells the people in there to leave, including a Captain. He tells me this time." I'm going to have to notify the Angry Intervention unit," [this job has something for everybody] again I tell him," let me tell you this, you do what you gotta do," and I leave.

The next day I'm in the Muster room with the other police officers, the Inspector comes in and says," Cimino how's it going," I tell him, "I'm taking back the streets," he smiles and leaves.

I had a feeling I knew who the two cops were. Those were the two that I thought didn't like me. I remember I saw one of the cops that I thought it was. He was walking down the hall of the precinct, a big guy gets behind him and gives him a kick in the ass that would have rattles my teeth. I'm pretty sure word got around that they ratted and that was pay back. And remember if that happens again!

Again, more of the guys that I used to work with started showing themselves. Thanks guys, nice to be remembered. These were all day tours that I did for Operation Take Back, that's because I was at the pound on a detail doing day tours.

They gave me this post a distance away from the precinct, so I always walked there, I get to a corner, and I see this guy on the opposite side; again I knew that he was going to be trouble. He comes over to me, and says," I just got out of Kings County Hospital psyche ward", okay, I talked a little with him. I knew or I had the feeling he was sizing me up, that day, okay, no problem. I go on post again. Another day, I spotted him on one of the blocks. I saw him go behind one of these huge hedges, near one of the houses, and he's hiding. I stayed on the same side of the block where the hedges are. As I'm about to pass, he jumps out, hands in the air and yelling. As soon as he did that, I throw a forearm to the face, without touching him, he almost shit. His head came down, his chin to his chest; I put him in his place. Now it's my post, "don't let me see you around here again." P.S. If I would have hit him he would definitely been back in the hospital, show of strength. Can't fight the world, this time, good call, or tired of going to the G building.

The first time I saw that move was in the 77 precinct, I had a post on Eastern Parkway. I was standing in front of a building, learning against a fence. This guy comes running out of the entrance, screaming with his hands up in the air, like; I'm the big bad boogeyman. When I spotted him, he didn't recognize me, so I let him go through his act, he passed me by. I'm sure that's a scare tactic or intimidation and if you did respond, and nail him and take him down, hey what did I do. They could be locked up for discon or attempted assault, your call. But these asses don't realize what attempted assault is or a Dis-Con summons is. Anyway, this guy I recognized him. He was an auxiliary police office in the 61 or 63 precinct I used to work in years ago. I even remembered his name. I didn't say anything or mention it to him, because there are ears all around and he might be a target for being an auxiliary police officer and considered a snitch.

Another time I saw this tactic, was in the 71 precinct, on the Operation Take Back. There was dispute in one of the buildings I took the job, R.M.P. for a back-up, might have been two cars. I'm talking, settling the dispute I knew that one of the guys in the dispute didn't like the outcome. As we leave I'm walking behind, slow, the two teams leave. I get back out on the sidewalk, all the R.M.P.'s left the scene. Again, I'm about maybe, seventy five to hundred feet from the doorway I just came out of. I'm putting scratches in my memo book. The same guy that was in the dispute, this time wearing a tee shirt, pants no shoes, He comes charging at me, screaming again hands up in the air like big scary man. I turned, stand there, hand I my slapper. I didn't move. He stops about fifteen feet in front of me, puts his head down, and walks back to his building. Never can tell, maybe next time they will attack, nothing's set in stone.

The reason I mention this, it's like in martial arts, when a person yells or screams, his Chi gets strong and he builds up his or her internal energy and makes him or her get bigger and stronger for that moment. So its intimidation and strength at the same time, it's good for fighting and self defense. So now that they did it and I didn't nail them with the night stick or slapper, what do I do now, put your head down and walk away. I took my chance and called their bluff. And if a cop nailed them with his or her night stick or black jack. They have the right to charge them with attempted assault, or give them a D.A.T. or put them through the system. Again why didn't I, same reason why I didn't shoot the female psycho, who jumped into the R.M.P. window with two knives in her hands, judgment, quick thinking, you call it, at the time you do what you think is right. Then the Monday morning quarter backs come out, and tell you, you shoulda. Yep I shoulda put I didn't.

I'm in like a better part of the neighborhood. So I was walking around, I saw a pay phone and decided to give my wife at the time a call. I'm on the phone talking, when I see these two guys walking with bags and a boom box; they were being followed by a guy and his Doberman pincher. The guy with the dog was about twenty feet behind them; I told my ex that I have to get off the phone I think something is going down. She really didn't give a fuck because she never asked, what had happened or if I was ever hurt. I hang up the phone, the guy with the dog says," that those two, just broke into an apartment," so I started walking after them, the dogs behind me which I didn't trust the dog because he was getting a little too close. I call out for the two guys to stop. They turned around and throw the boom box at me, I moved and it hit the ground. The dogs growling and they start to run. I start chasing, I put it over the air I'm in pursuit of two perps who just did a burglary.

Central asks what's your location, as usual I don't remember the block I'm on, I tell her, I don't know, as I'm chasing them, I'm asking the people, as I pass," what block is this." no answer, these type of neighbors most don't want to get involved with the police because of retaliation. So I'm chasing them, asking the same question," what block am I on?" still no answer they go over a fence, I go over, now I'm on a different block. I'm hearing sirens, now the R.M.P.'s are searching. I see one coming down the block that I'm on. I have my hat off, they passed me by, I yell into the radio, "you just passed me," they stopped, and I jumped into the car.

Now we're searching, they put it over the air that they have the police officer, I really psyched, I tell them to stop the car, I'm better off on foot. I'm reading the people in the street, there like directing me to a certain apartment building. I go into this building. I'm followed by one team of police officers and one single cop, the single cop, I looked at him, I felt like, he might have my back He comes with me, the other team splits from us. We start going up the stairs, I see fresh footprints on the stairs could be theirs or anyone else's. We check the water closets, on all of the floors. If anyone ran up, nothing. Okay, I go back to the block where they dropped the loot, everything's gone. Nothing new, I figured, when the owners come back from where ever they went. They'll call the precinct, and make a report. I went back to the phone to see if the quarter was in the box, again no luck, story of my life. :]

They gave me this foot post, but before I went out one of the cops told me, you had better be careful, two plain-clothes cops, were jumped and beaten up on that block. I asked him, if they took back the block, no answer. So I guess they didn't understand. They gave me that post for a week or more. I walked down that block and I knew something wasn't right, I saw some characters sitting on stoops, just my gut feeling. So the next day I walk down the same block, this is where the two plainclothes cops were jumped. This time I walked down the blocked with me gun in my hand. I know I had an attitude or it was given to me. I saw the same character, so I started to talk out loud to myself " ok mother fuckers you want to play I ready," and walk up and down the street with my gun in hand, you do what you got to do at the time you're doing it. Next day same thing, than I saw a change, some people started coming out of their houses and passing me by, they wouldn't look at me and mumbling in a low voice, nice job officer, good job and the shits that were hanging out were gone. This time when I got to near the end of the block I think it was a Taylor shop, he called me in and started yelling and talking loud, in between the yells he was giving me information on drug dealers, he did that because if the wrong person saw he would be dead. I went back to the precinct and made out an intelligence report.

I was there again, standing near this grocery store, this young kid starts talking to me, maybe in his late teens, early twenties, he had two friends with him. I knew he was show boating, and I felt he was bad, but I was just visiting that precinct so I didn't know what was what. He left with his boys. Then some Rastafarian was standing in the middle of the street looking for a stare down with me, I mean, what fucking balls. I'm pissed, I went to the street, again, took my gun out and said," Ok fuck, want to do it lets do it," he looked and walk away fast. I figure I must be having a good day. I mean, these people do not give a shit about cops or people or anyone. Sounds like my ex. But these guys I don't have to sleep with.

I did the post again, I was standing there. Plainclothes cops stops their car, there from warrants. They said there looking for this guy and show me a picture, guess who, you're right, the kid was showing boating with his two friends in front of the store.

Another Rastafarian thought he was king of the block, I told him next time I see him he better have a fucking gun; he moved on, I don't know I might have been having another good day, or having a better choice of words, then please and excuse me. Walking with no attitude or need a better vocabulary.

They put me on Utica avenue and. I was warned by some cops that there were these two buildings, apartment buildings, maybe five stories, one across from each other. A lot of drug dealers, and they said every once in I while, they would have a shoot out, so watch out. The first day I walked my beat, walking up and down, stopping in stores, in this area cops would not be welcomes account of the corruption, but I did it anyway, just to show the people that were trying to earn an honest living that, maybe I was here for a good reason. Next day I did the same. I think the people and the store owners were starting to get used to seeing me. And that I was there the whole tour, I even ate on the avenue. I stopped in one of the stores; I think it might have been a shoemaker. The owner was behind the counter, told me about those building that the cops told me about, his store was close by, and he showed me bullet holes in his walls. I said thanks for the tip, and moved on.

Another tour there and I'm walking this time the atmosphere is very different, no one on the street, the doors to the stores were closed not locked. This time I saw more Rastafarians on the street, so I walked my post. I walked up to Utica Avenue and Eastern Parkway, and the people weren't responding to me as usual, I felt the fear. So I'm walking back up the post and I see this Rastafarian and a girl standing on one of the corners, like he owned the place. I spotted one Rastafarian on one of the fire escapes looking at me, and the couple on the street. The stores owners were in their stores, but their doors were closed, no people walking the streets. So I'm looking at this guy, he has his arms folded across his chest with a big smile on his face, like he was king, the girl standing there at his side. I knew it was time to take back my blocks.

So I walked across to where he was. I looked at him. And I tell him, "now you see, if you stand here and I stand here, they might think, that you owned the block," as I'm talking to him, I'm watching the guy on the fire escape. Then I say "So one of us is going to have to go, and I know it's not going to be me." This time his girl moves away, and he keeps looking, and I keep looking. I am trying to make him bow out gracefully. He looks smiles and walks away. So he left, I stayed, and the Avenue went back to what I call, for this neighborhood, normal. It's my post. Stores doors opened and people back on the streets. But I still won't call it Mr. Rogers's neighborhood.

Still the same day, as I took back my block, I'm leaning against the wall, I don't remember how long after. I hear shots coming from those two building. I'm maybe a block and a half away. When I hear Central," shots fired at," you guessed it, said location, I put over the air, "Central this is patrol post so and so, confirmed shots fired, I'm responding," Central comes back. "Wait for back-up." When I get there, so does multiply radio cars. They go through the building. On one of the side blocks of one of the building, I spotted this Day Care Center with two adults and all the kids outside in the back of their building, right where there is a shoot out. I went to that location, and told them to move in side for now; I didn't tell them what was happening. After a while, the cops came down no arrests, just normal for that area. I think from there I got in one of the cars drove back to the precinct had meal then went back to post. I don't remember how long I stayed there. When working mothers have no choice, wow, day care center?

Just a point of information I mentioned this. when I was a rookie and they labeled this police officer a coward, this guy I drove with was my partner for the day, Hey I don't know, and I don't listen to rumors, unless I know firsthand, But anyway that was what ten or more years ago. When I went to the 71 precinct, I'm getting a radio, and Who do you think is giving out radios, yep it was him, he looks at me, I look at him, I knew he remembered me just by his eyes, and flashbacks of what they labeled him. Thanks for the radio. We moved on. This might be a repeat saying, wouldn't be the first time I made a mistake over and over and over.

From the 71 precinct they transferred me to the 69 precinct, which is in Brooklyn, Canarsie section of Brooklyn. The first day my sense of humor didn't go over well with the desk officer, which was a lieutenant, he gave me a look, and I also had a feeling that a phone call was made with this move. So they gave me a foot post, and for some reason I was getting scratched more than usual, and it was this lieutenant. I met this other police officer who used to work in the 112 precinct. He had a dealing with this lieutenant and for some unknown reason I stood up for this cop. So we had to call the P.B.A. Delegate down. The young cop, he was nervous, so I waited with him. When the delegate came down, I'm pretty sure I recognized him. He talked to us, mostly the police officer form the 112 precinct, because I don't think I really gave a fuck, it was such bullshit. I was tired of waiting, while he talked to the boss that made the stink, so I left. I didn't know how it turned out. They didn't notify me so I figured; it was squashed at precinct level.

From there they shipped me to the Bronx, which could be the reason I didn't hear from them, Brooklyn to the Bronx, the 50 precinct. See I believe when you love the job your doing, everything becomes part of the job even the bullshit, so it doesn't bother you as much. So now, I'm traveling to the Bronx every day. I'm driving on the Mosholu Parkway if they didn't tell me about that Parkway; I would have never known it existed.

When I get to the precinct, Roll Call gives me the new posts list. They give me this avenue, don't remember the name but I'm there standing foot post. I start figuring out who the people are that you might have to watch a little more than others.

The days that I'm at the precinct, I met the night watch commander, hey Al, "how you doing," he was in charge of the Detectives in the 112 precinct. Now he was in the Bronx, "doing fine, here you know Operation Takes Back." "Hey, nice seeing you." When I got to this precinct, I always dressed out of my car trunk in the parking lot. I guess the Inspector saw me from his window, because either a police officer or a sergeant came over to me, and said, "The inspector told me to get you a locker." So now, I had a locker.

I remember one day standing in the 124 room or complaint room. This civilian is mopping the floor. Again, there were many young cops there. Two police officers came in with a collar. The guy washing the floor tells them, nasty," don't come in, go through the back, the floor is wet," the fucking desk officer doesn't say a thing, and these two cops are going to walk around the precinct outside with their prisoner, and I know from other incidents That, it takes a second for something to go wrong. So I come out, and tell them, you don't listen to this guy, come in and bring him this way, like fuck him. The civilian is pissed; the cops came in through the front and walk on his wet floor. No way to make friends, and influence people, not here to make friends just made in safer.

So from there I started to get foot posts further and further away from the precinct, and this time I feel like I'm being followed. Because I start getting scratches from this Irish Captain and my gut is telling me this guy looks like he has it in for me; possible, could have gotten a phone call from the lieutenant at the Whitestone pound, or he was in charge of the wet floor squad. So now, I think my balls are being broken.

I don't usually call the union delegate; I must have used them three times in twenty years, with no results. So I make a phone call. It happens that the P.B.A. delegate from the pound was a police officer I went to the Academy with and he was one of the guys I hung out with. So I tell him I think there breaking my balls,

I tell him what I noticed and what I thought the lieutenant at the pound was doing. So again I said that he was taking all the Irish cops off Operation Take Back and putting all the Italians on the street. And I'm being shipped from one place to another, and the cop I'm talking to is all Irish. Real nice person from the time I met him, matter of fact, all the guys I think, except me, were Irish from the Police Academy, nice crew. When I get back to the pound the next day, the delegate was there, and I was off the detail, and back at the pound. This time the phone call worked. Thanks.

BACK AT THE POUND

I remember I was standing in the in-take room when the lieutenant, peeks his head in, same smile. Now remember all or most of the guys are afraid of him. I see the expressions change on the guy's faces, because indirectly or directly he used to threaten them and myself included. The guys that were on details and are afraid to lose their detail and the guys that had heavy clouds over their heads, they're either going to lose their job or worse going to get locked-up. He used to really needle them. So, I'm standing there. He comes in, and he is standing on the other side of this what looked like a small podium where you would sign in or sign out the vehicles. I said." you know Lou, you're a crazy mother fucker; if we were both in the street they wouldn't have a chance." He looked at me, said nothing, and walked out. I'm sure that was the reason he invited me to the Jamaican day parade, he would also be there. One of the worse parade's in the city, because of the crime that happens that day. It's party time.

Whitestone pound motorcycle detail

I remember they implemented a computer system at the pound and everyone had to take lessons, I think it was between one to three hour course. We had to go to the College Point trailer. College Point is another place where the P.D. stores vehicles, and would become the new pound. So it was my turn, I bitched, I went there, they showed me what I had to do. I must have stayed for at least ten minutes; I told them they could train a monkey in doing this. I don't think the people that had this job like what I said, I was bored shit. I walked out went back to the Whitestone pound, the sergeant said what are you doing back, I said serge, again they could train a monkey in doing this job I got bored, Al go back to the bikes. Okay

I was at the Whitestone pound for a while when they asked me if I wanted to take care of the motorcycles. That consisted of taking in the bikes that were stolen, damaged, account of an accident, taken off the owner because he didn't have the right paperwork and until he brought his or her ownership down we would keep it, and then after a certain amount of time the bikes would be auctioned off.

We had this walk behind hi-low, well let me tell you about the person before me, the first that I remember was that police officer who found that dog trained him as a guard dog and he bit me. The other guy was a police officer from Manhattan, he had the Central Park detail or post, a Viet Nam veteran, he told me he and five or six men like himself would be the first to go into the jungle and they would boo-be trap the jungle, serious, but at the pound friendly, likeable real nice personality. He was taken off for some reason or another and I took over.

So every day the bikes came in and I would use this hi-low, pick up the bikes place them in the cage. This machine would either get stuck or break down so much, that I stopped using it, either I would carry or drag these bike, some of them weighting between three to five hundred pounds. Speaking for myself, it felt great because there was no gym there and I was used to working out every day, so this made me feel very good.

Once a month they would give me the paperwork on the bikes that were going to auction. I would pull the bikes and set up the auction, always gave them more than what they expected, putting a four hour day into eight hours was tough, so I did a lot of extra work and fast. I couldn't just sit around and pretend I was working, or going into the other trailer and watch TV.

One of the sergeants that worked there, came over to me and said Al start getting rid of any bikes, paper work or not, even if someone owns them. "No way. "A short time after that the lieutenant calls me into his office. I don't remember what he said, but I told him this sergeant [name] is telling me to get rid of any bike owned or not, and don't worry about the paperwork. So he calls the sergeant into his office and tells him in front of me what I said. The sergeant says," I never told him that", I didn't say anything I gave him a look and walked out. That sergeant was his buddy to, nothing ever came of it, but I did the bikes my way.

I remember I got a motorcycle for safekeeping they told me this was the bike that, the owner of it, was from one of the Hells Angels gangs. The story in the paper was. There was a traffic accident, an off duty police officer and this bad dude, the cop shows his gun, the member on bike stabs him and kills him. The defense was the police officer never identified himself and it was self-defense. The guy beat the rap. So after the case was over, these two guys have to go to release, that's the name of the other section from intake. No one tells me anything. So I'M in the bike cage, I see these two guys coming in. I didn't know who they were, but I knew they were bad, very bad news. They gave me the release paperwork. I go get the bike; I recognized the bike and put two and two together. I can tell you these guys walk in fear and in hell every day. Scary.

As I said, I was doing the work for the bikes so fast that my days were mine. I guess the bosses and the other police officers who use to do that work; they were getting upset, because they were jerking the bosses, around, complaining, there's so much work, and so little time. They started making me do other jobs; I really didn't give a fuck, because this went on whatever precinct I worked in. They gave me a job, I did the job and moved on, but always fast, hated to waste time. Cops got pissed, civilians got pissed, like I said four hours into eight hours lot of time to kill, couldn't do it. So you win some you lose some. That police officer who was the Viet Nam veteran wanted the bike position back, so I moved on. It was no big deal for me to move on.

I remember I used to talk to one of the police woman, black girl very nice, she was trying to get out on three quarters, something to do with her hand. I guess she spoke to her husband about me because every time he would visit I would get bad vibes from him. One day on one of my walks, around the Whitestone Pound, I was crossing the street from an overpass and this van makes a left turn and chased me onto the side walk, I recognized the van. So when I got back to the pound I told her you know your husband tried to run me down, she looked didn't say anything, but when I retired, she finally got her three quarters and invited me to her retirement party, I didn't go but sent her a basket, why spoil the fun.

There was another police woman, she was a sergeant who got demoted and sent to the pound. She was setting up her case for getting back her stripes. Tall thin girl, blonde, pretty, for some reason, I think we became friends. I use to break her balls. She used to come in and clean the intake room, I used to tell her after your finished you can start with the windows. "fuck you Al," I said," we're cops not cleaning people," guess the bosses heard and they started me sweeping the floors, again no big thing. We talked about her case in getting her job back, and other stuff. When my brother died, she took up a collection, sent a basket to my house and sent flowers to the funeral parlor. I didn't expect it and was deeply touched. When I retired I heard from the grape vine she had a baby, didn't know if it was true or they were just breaking her balls again, they said it was a girl, female single parent. I think about her and miss her too. She was one of my favorites. Never found out if she got her stripes back, hope she did.

Another guy at the pound was there under an investigation. I think he was from the 71 or the 75 precinct, tall, nice looking guy, but real bad guy. He and his boys, they said, were doing from five thousand to ten thousand a week or a month, from drugs and other stuff.

He used to come to the pound dress in a full-length leather coat, driving a new corvette. One day I asked him, oh, he also had a big house on Long Island. "Hey [name] do you have a second job," he said," no", I said," you come to the pound in, what an eight hundred dollar leather coat drive a new corvette, on a cops salary." Next day he comes in wearing a denim jacket and driving a beat up Honda. The job nailed him, he did some heavy time. He's probably out by now.

While at the pound, I went on a few details. One was a Jamaican demonstration I went with this one police officer. The one I suspected of cutting my tire. They stationed us on one of the blocks, right where the demo was taken place. I ran into my old partner from the 77 precinct, the black female, I saw her, she made detective, I didn't say anything, she came over, said," how are you?" "I see you got the shield," small talk and that was it. I'm standing there, and I'm listening to the rebel rousers that were speaking, saying, hey they say it's a free country and freedom of speech, this guy is yelling into the mike," we have to kill all whites" so on and so forth, I know it bothered me, but that's the job.

The other detail was the Beijing demonstration in Manhattan, that's, when the Asians had a demo in I think it was China and a student was killed at that demonstration, I think he was standing in front of a tank. So they had one in Manhattan for, I guess a tribute. So when I got there, this time I was the only one from the pound to be sent. We lined up on a corner; I was in the first row and the Chief of Manhattan is talking to us.

He's right in front of me, and he's saying," if anyone, spits, hits or throws things at you, you just stand there and do nothing," I looked at him and said," listen if anyone hits or spits at me or another cop he going down." He says." okay you, I want you in the barriers for the eights hour," low and behold, I was put where the stage was. I had no clue who would be there; I was put right in the heart of the demonstration.

So now there are barriers circling the stage, the stage is like in the middle of this enclosed area. The back and sides walls of the stage are made of a black material. Myself I always try to stay out of the crowd.

First, I see the mayor of New York coming in the enclosed barriers. I could have touched him. Then I started to see the New York Senators and Assemblymen, hey nice. With the mayor, I see his bodyguards. Before that I'm looking around and I see the people in charge of the demo constantly looking at me than looking away, I look they looked. I figured, account of the Beijing demo they didn't trust anyone in uniform.

One particular girl, was looking at me more than usual, and I know it wasn't for my looks, learned that young, she looked like she was one of the persons who organized this demo and was in charge. So I'm standing there. A person in plain clothes comes over to me. He says," I want you to move those people, if they start trouble, there like professional agitators," I said," who you are?" I'm a police officer, working for, he was like a liaison for the demonstrators and the police department, I said," see this" police officer, I pointed to his shield, do it yourself, he walked away. I recognized him from working at the 77 precinct, he use to work there, when I was there. I didn't let him know, he might have even recognized me. I don't know.

So while I was there. These agitators, I think one girl and three guys they came in a Volkswagen bug. I spotted the car they came out of. There standing there in front of the crowd. I think they were almost in front of the barricades, making noise. I see this same Asian girl looking at me again. She looked nervous. So I walked over to them, I told the leader who was the girl. I'll give you five minutes, [that was my thing I always said,] if you're not out of here in five minutes you'll be arrested. That's what I told her, I think I heard her say, "This guy's not playing". I looked at my watch, walked a short distance away, she look at me and then looked at her guys, she gave them like a nod and they left. From there the Asian girl attitude changed, because awhile later she called me over to do something or help her with something. I guessed she started to trust me I was there as always, to do my job.

So when all the big shots were finally in and settled, everyone was in front of the stage even the body guards, me I stayed in the back, facing the back of the stage, I was at the right hand corner in the rear of the stage. I see this Asian, around maybe five foot four to five foot six, thin hair and mustache, standing in back of the stage, on the ground. He was standing center of the curtain wall. He has a pouch on his waist. He's facing the back wall of the stage, he's all alone. I see him go into a soft bow stance and reach for his pouch, he started to open it. I knew when I wore my pouch and went into that soft bow stance, I was going for my gun. I run up to him, put my gun to his head, he starts yelling, camera, camera. I check the pouch; he leaves like a bat out of hell. So what, are you taking pictures of the curtain?

I said to myself, nice all the body guards are in front, no one spread out and was taking care of the rear. From that, I started seeing them move around from the front and start spreading out. That might have been the first time I ever put my gun to a person's head, hopefully the last.

It was a good day. When I saw the Mayor, he has some presence, big person, nice appearance. Oh that was MAYOR KOCH.

I'm sure either the lieutenant was getting to me, or I was getting to him. So one day he calls me into his office, I go in, sit down, he's behind his desk sitting, feet up on the desk. He says," I bet you want to get up and punch me in the face". I looked at him, stand up, put my hands on his desk, lean over and say, "No, I want to take my gun out, put it to your head and blow your brain out, the reason I'm not going to do it, is because I like you. Then I walk out, around a month later he retired. I don't know, did you ever, just have one of those days?

Sometime after I decided to retire. I called my friend I knew at the Pension Section and he made it an easy transition for me.

The people at the Pound threw me a retirement party, which I was totally surprised and honored. One of the Police Officer's wives' made a banner congratulating me on my retirement, another surprise; I still have the banner and memories. Thanks to all.

Just more bits of info. I had a friend who was an undercover police officer, during the Kappa Commission. He knew a lot of organize crime people, talk to them friendly and so on. He was arrested and sent to prison for three years, he never gave up anyone. So he did the time. He told me when he was in prison he met the boys that he knew on the street, they knew him, for them, jail time. Was like a vacation, they did and ate whatever they felt like. He use to be invited to eat with them, veal parmigiana, eggplant parmigiana, baked ziti, whatever. So it was hard on his family, but he said it wasn't that bad for special sorts of people. Good to know people in high and low places, good contacts.

Another cop I worked with was a correction officer. He said the same thing years later, when he became a New York City Police Officer, the boys were treated like kings and they got whatever they wanted.

Just showing and telling two sides of the coin. The police Department is like a big department store. The big department Stores have a column that says they expect the workers to steal maybe three to five percent, anything more than that, than they do an investigations and firing. Same thing with the Police department, they know cops are going to do wrong, but when it gets out of hand or you're bringing attention to the department, now they have to act. Also most of the police officer that became bosses and were doing bad thing as Police Officers, the cops that knew them and were caught, and these Police Officers that became bosses and were told about the certain corruption, and were still in the-grape vine with the bad guy, this information tinkles down to the right people, who can tell these guys that are doing wrong, that there's was going to be an investigation, so if they don't get the message, then you're caught. Maybe a word to the wise should be sufficient, but some cops think it can't happen to them, and then reality sets in. Here comes another Oh shit. And sometimes it's a no win situation. Not all cops and bosses are like this I've met some great bosses and cops, and met some of the shit as well.

Again small bit of information, and easy talking. When I was in the 77 precinct, there was a female Anti Crime police office there. On a four by twelve she came over to me and my partner, and asked me that they were going sky diving, asked me if I wanted to go, and told her hey not for me, don't want to get killed.

Well some years later I made the jump twice, not tandem, solo, the second time the parachute mal functioned, the two end tubes failed to inflate, this was twelve weeks later after the five hour class, of teaching if the parachute fails in certain ways these are the things you have to do. Well when that happened, things do come back, and I had to correct the situation three thousand feet in the air, safe landing. The first jump he says, [that's the instructor, I was the first out of the plane on both occasions,] "see that red X on the ground, that's where you're supposed to land," I tell him "most times I drove my car and look for a location I get lost, and you expect me to find that X?". Wonder if they ever jumped, the ones from the 77preicnct, and the one who invited me to sky dive. Oh yea, they do make you wear helmets. Also did a three hundred foot bungy jump, also a helmet. :]

I'll say one thing. For every bad cop there's one the job, and the ones you work with, bad or, the so called empty suits, there's fifty or hundred times that ready and willing to do the job and give their life for the safety of the city and the people they're protecting.

As for myself, I did the job, made mistakes, learned from them. Learned from other Police Officers mistakes, and what other older Police Officers said, to enlighten me with their words and wisdom, to make my job better and the hard times easier. These guys that I met through the twenty years of working, it was my pleasure to have worked and to have known them. Something you don't want to forget.

Over the twenty years as a Police Officer and the handling of thousands of job. This is what made me the person I am today and the kind of thinking that comes with it, which whether or not you realize it, will stay with me for the rest of my life. It didn't give me the cynical way of looking at life, because this I refused to accept, because then what's the use, But more of a protective way to keep myself and my friends safer.